BUZZIE AND THE BULL

Buzzie and the Bull

A GM, *a* Clubhouse Favorite, *and the* Dodgers' 1965 Championship Season

Ken LaZebnik
Foreword by Bob Bavasi

UNIVERSITY OF NEBRASKA PRESS • LINCOLN

To three beloved Dodger fans in my life:
my wife, Kate, and our sons, Jack and Ben

Contents

Illustrations

14. Headshot of Al Ferrara
15. Buzzie Bavasi throws out the ceremonial first pitch
16. Al “the Bull” Ferrara delighting an audience of children

Foreword

Bob Bavasi

"He's a good guy to have on the club."

And with that simple sentiment, Al "the Bull" Ferrara was again playing Major League Baseball.

It was 1971. I was in high school on spring break and about to walk back to the team hotel from the San Diego Padres spring training facility. My dad saw me and said, "Wait with me. I'll be leaving soon."

I waited in the back corner of the conference room at Desert Sun Stadium in Yuma, Arizona, and watched something I had never seen: the coaches, scouts, and my dad, Buzzie Bavasi, who was the team president, making the club before breaking camp.

The better players made the team without discussion. Then came guys on the bubble. Whom to keep? Whom to release? For each of these players there were plenty of stat-filled, pointed, and sometimes heated arguments.

I had had no favorite player until a year earlier, when I decided to pledge my allegiance to the Bull. And the Bull was now next on the block. Would he make the club or finally have to get a real job?

Somebody said, "He's a good guy to have on the club." Then came a lot of head nodding. And that was that. For an eighth season, Al "the Bull" Ferrara was again in the big leagues. Five seasons with the Los Angeles Dodgers and now this, his third, with the San Diego Padres.

I was stunned. No stats. No arguments. No heated discussions.

Nothing but a simple, "He's a good guy to have on the club" got the Bull a spot in the big leagues.

They went over so many players in such great detail; why was there nothing of the sort with the Bull? If I had been at all inquisitive, I would have asked my dad on the drive back to the hotel. At the time I was not at all inquisitive.

Buzzie died on May 1, 2008. My oldest brother, Peter, took up the task of answering Dad's correspondence. A year or so after Dad's passing, Peter said to me, "I've been having a lot of fun keeping up with the players by email. And Ferrara is really something. He sends Mom a handwritten note each month."

"What a guy," I said. "You know he's my favorite player."

"What!" Peter said. "You grew up around the Dodgers—Koufax, Drysdale, and the rest—and you pick Ferrara as your favorite player?"

What can I say? I liked the Bull. He came off the bench hard. He was all business on the field. When I was around him, he made me feel like a million bucks, and I was just a kid walking through the clubhouse once in a while.

But what did Buzzie see in him to have him on eight of his teams? Buzzie was the president or general manager of every team on which the Bull started for those eight seasons. In baseball parlance these were "Buzzie's clubs." Buzzie made the final call on which players made the roster. Well, I suppose not the final call. For much of Buzzie's baseball tenure that final say belonged to Walter O'Malley, the Dodgers owner, who employed Buzzie to essentially play baseball cards for a living. As long as Buzzie adhered to the budget that Mr. O'Malley set, he was free to make the roster. What a great deal.

So what was it about the Bull that kept him in the big leagues far longer than the average player? What kept him from falling off the bubble and out of the game? Was it his stats? Baseball has always been statistics-driven. The Dodgers had the best stats of their day. The first full-time statistician in the game, Allan Roth, was with the Dodgers, and he gave Buzzie the most exceptional statistics available. My father didn't ignore those stats. But stats by themselves are one-dimensional. They become far more useful when used by a skilled practitioner in the understanding of human nature and the intangible benefits that a player may offer.

Perhaps what kept the Bull in the big leagues was something intangible: a quality of his personality that encompassed nerves of steel, camaraderie, courage, and playing hard every moment he was on the field. These are the intangibles that caused his teammates to vote him a full World Series share in 1965, even when the Bull hadn't played a complete season.

Today, with baseball's obsession with statistical analysis and data-driven decision making, we may have lost the wisdom that comes from focusing not only on a player's numbers, but also on his heart. The Bull's teammate, Ron Fairly, summed up what Al Ferrara brought to the 1965 Dodgers—and what his general manager, my father, understood in his bones as he sought out players with the heart to win a championship: "There's no stat for that."

One can easily identify at least one game that Al Ferrara won for the Dodgers during the 1965 season. It was a key win in a season in which but two games made the difference between their clinching a pennant and their landing in another playoff. But how many wins were also nurtured by the intangibles that Ferrara brought to the clubhouse? How does one measure that?

This book chronicles a friendship between two very different men. But they were joined by a belief that baseball games are won not just by players who produce statistical success, but also by those who play the game with nerves of steel, with love, and with heart.

Acknowledgments

Bob Bavasi is responsible for the genesis of this book, introducing me to his favorite player—Al "the Bull" Ferrara—and suggesting there was a book in the story of the Bull's unlikely friendship with his father, Dodger general manager Buzzie Bavasi. Bob has shepherded this project over the past several years in every way conceivable: arranging for over a year of interviews with Ferrara; bringing his brothers together to reminisce; gathering photographs; reaching out to the current Dodger organization; and working tirelessly in a hundred other ways. This book would not exist without him and the support of his wife, Margaret Bavasi, who compiled the beautiful letters that Buzzie mailed home from World War II. Peter Bavasi has been invaluable in his recollections, comments, and suggestions for improving the manuscript. Bill Bavasi and Chris Bavasi also made valuable suggestions and offered memories.

During several years of regular interviews Al "the Bull" Ferrara has been unfailingly honest, open, and hilarious. His generosity to me is mirrored in his generosity to the community around him, both on the field during his playing days and now off the field as he works as a Dodger ambassador to schools, community organizations, and youth baseball activities. The Bull radiates positive energy wherever he goes, and I am thankful to have had the chance to join in the wide circle of his admirers. I am grateful to Kay Donno for her unflagging support of this project, graciously opening her home to me and offering her own recollections.

Thank you to all those who agreed to be interviewed for this book. They represent a trove of baseball history. Particular thanks to Bob Case, Tommy Davis, Ron Fairly, Wes Parker, Ron Perranoski, and Tom Villante.

Liz Van Hoose gave brilliant counsel to the shaping of the manuscript in an early and crucial phase. Mark Langill, historian of the Los Angeles Dodgers, generously reviewed the manuscript, offered his expertise to me and Bob Bavasi, and was immensely helpful in facilitating our search for photographs.

Assembling and getting permissions for the photographs was its own arduous task. Bob Bavasi headed this task up with his usual expertise. For the photos, thanks to Jon Chapper, assistant director, public relations, Los Angeles Dodgers, for his help in obtaining photo releases from the club. Thanks to William Swank and Andy Strasberg for assistance in identifying San Diego Padres–era photographs. Thanks to Keith Kesler, social media librarian for the Los Angeles Public Library, for help with the LA Reads photos.

Thank you to Rob Taylor, the superb editor at the University of Nebraska Press, as well as Courtney Ochsner and the entire team there for their support and devotion to excellence. It is much appreciated.

And thanks go, as always, to my family for their support over the years of seeing this book to publication: my wife, Kate, and our sons, Jack and Ben, true Dodger fans all.

Introduction

On February 28, 1965, the Los Angeles Dodgers opened spring training at Dodgertown, a self-contained baseball world built from an old naval air station in Vero Beach, Florida. Six hundred players lived together in barracks, ate in the same cafeteria, and were roused at 7 a.m. by the team's eccentric Mr. Fixit, Herman Levy, who stalked between the bunks blowing a whistle. Levy, a squat little man who had worked for the Brooklyn post office before being hired as a devoted jack-of-all-trades for the Dodgers, then raised the American flag over the compound. With the stars and stripes blowing in the Florida wind, he recited the Pledge of Allegiance in a stentorian Brooklyn accent that would wake the dead.

Later that morning, after the group breakfast, General Manager Emil "Buzzie" Bavasi wandered among the players as they stretched out on the green grass. He joked with the veterans, needled the rounders on his team, and in the process confirmed what everyone had done the night before. The whole camp was aware that Buzzie magically knew everything that transpired in and around Dodgertown. Bavasi had an intelligence pipeline that ran through the clubhouse guys, the scouts, and the coaches. Bavasi paused before one of his favorite players. It wasn't Sandy Koufax or Don Drysdale or Maury Wills. While he loved his great stars for their athletic talents, there was one player Bavasi treasured because he played with the same 110 percent commitment that he brought to creating a memorable evening along the Sunset

Strip. Al "the Bull" Ferrara was a man who carried a party in his back pocket. On the field Ferrara had a ferocious intensity, but savoring the midnight streets of Los Angeles or New York or Chicago, in the midst of strippers, horse players, female bullfighters, baseball Annies, and barmaids, the Bull sprouted a garden of joy. He had the gregarious character of a Brooklyn blue-collar native; the fields on which he grew up playing baseball were the streets outside his family's Brooklyn apartment. Ferrara was the last Brooklyn native to come up through the old Dodger system of the "Dodger Rookies" team; he was pure Brooklyn—loyal, joyous, a man with a million friends. Those friends were all around him now, fellow Dodgers loosening up on the warm Florida grass. Fellow Brooklyn native Tommy Davis was joking about riding the IRT, a subway line only he and Ferrara were familiar with among this new generation of Dodgers. Ferrara cracked up his roommate and running buddy Johnny Podres; he cracked up all of his teammates, and he did so in the best way: he was enthusiastic and encouraging, one of those players with an instinct for keeping a clubhouse loose. The Bull never thought for an instant about storing his grain for the winter of his life; he lived in the moment and by the crazy dictum of "Ferraranomics": the art of piling up debt and then brilliantly dodging paying up. As Ferrara said many years later, "If there was an off-the-field Hall of Fame, I'd get in on the first ballot." He never held anything back, on or off the field, and this fearless quality of commitment was what won ball games. Buzzie knew this and embraced it. On this spring morning in 1965, the Bull was stretching, working out the kinks of a hangover.

"Whatcha do last night, Al?"

"I was in my room, Buzzie."

The entire team broke into laughter.

"Come on, Al," Buzzie persisted, "What'd you do?"

"I enjoyed myself with the local flora and fauna. I started off at this bar . . ."

Most general managers wouldn't ask the question. Most players wouldn't tell the truth. To GMs, players were guys they would trade like they would trade baseball cards. Getting close to the players, knowing them as flesh and blood human beings, would only get in the way of business. GMs of that era sold players to other teams, traded them, and set their salaries with impunity. The men who played the game were bodies that produced certain results on the field, and a GM's job was to find the best bodies his team owner could afford. But Buzzie Bavasi was different. He had a radically different notion of how to build a championship team: he sought out players with nerves of steel.

For Buzzie a player's psychological make-up was as important as his athleticism. From the top to the bottom, Bavasi made fearless players into the links of a solid Dodger chain. Anyone can identify a superstar. Buzzie's genius was to fill the bottom of his roster with winners. That's how he won games and pennants. He looked for guys with the guts of burglars who would never get scared in the clutch. He had to because the Dodgers were built on pitching and speed and defense, and they won tight games, 1–0 and 3–2 and 2–1. In 1965 they led the league in one-run games—60 of the 154 games they played that year were decided by just one run. Hence every game was a clutch game. Finding players at the bottom of the roster who could win one or two of those games made the difference between a pennant winner and an also-ran. Al Ferrara was not an everyday player. But he was the sort of player who competed ferociously and over the course of the 1965 season was responsible for at least one crucial Dodger win in that season's pennant race that the Dodgers won by just two games. Buzzie knew how to identify those singular players who won on the field but also contributed through their personality off the field. Clubhouse chemistry can come from the conviction of fearlessness. As a young Minor League general manager he had witnessed such fearlessness firsthand when Jackie Robinson broke the color line. In 1965, a year of uncertainty in which American society was torn by a growing war in Vietnam and a surging divide at home, Bavasi looked for a team that would never flinch. And Al "the Bull" Ferrara was the epitome of a man with no fear.

The situation was never going to overpower the Bull. This was the only Major League baseball player who played classical piano in concert at Carnegie Hall when he was sixteen. Moxie was part of his DNA. In Vero Beach, as Ferrara regaled his boss with tales of the previous night's madness, he only reinforced Buzzie's belief that here was a ballplayer with balls. Who else would let his employer know how poorly he took care of himself off the field?

That February day was the beginning of a season that unfolded as a crazy roller-coaster ride. The 1965 baseball journey encompassed a thrilling pennant race settled on the final day of the season, a city engulfed in flames, a perfect game, and a legendary general manager who extolled his friend the Bull as a hero in May and then banished him from the team in July in the depths of a public purgatory. Both men emerged tempered by the fire. The marriage of these two characters—the general manager who valued fearlessness above all else and the crazy player who loved living on the edge—became the embodiment of champions who never choked in the clutch. Buzzie Bavasi's record towers above his contemporaries. In seventeen years as the Dodgers GM, his teams won eight pennants and four World Series titles. He did it with a plan. His approach deserves recognition, and his friendship with Al "the Bull" Ferrara illustrates the ground upon which he staked his baseball career. The summer of 1965 proved Buzzie Bavasi's thesis that champions are built on players with one core characteristic: nerves of steel.

BUZZIE AND THE BULL

The Winter of 1964   **1**

In December 1964 Buzzie Bavasi and the Los Angeles Dodgers faced a serious problem. They had lost badly that season, finishing in sixth place, with a record below .500. This was a team that had won the 1963 World Series in triumphant fashion, sweeping its old rivals, the New York Yankees, and seemed destined to take over the Yankees' mantle as baseball's greatest dynasty. Then they fell on their faces in 1964. Buzzie Bavasi was determined to bring them back to greatness. The Dodgers, after all, had been part of the triangle of magnificent New York teams that had defined Major League baseball in the 1950s. The Yankees, the Dodgers, and the Giants had been intracity rivals and champions. Between 1949 and 1958 there had been only one year that a New York team had not won the World Series. Then baseball shifted its focus from New York City to the West Coast. Along with the Dodgers and Giants, America's center of gravity shifted from the boroughs of New York City to the carefree counties of Los Angeles and San Francisco.

The Dodgers were a legendary team from a legendary place, and when they moved west in 1958, Bavasi performed the remarkable feat of winning another World Series in 1959. He transformed the team from the power-hitting Dodgers of cozy Ebbets Field to the power-pitching Dodgers of Koufax and Drysdale. How does a GM do that? And what, in a larger sense, constitutes the GM's job? In 1967 *Los Angeles Times* writer Charles Maher described Bavasi's salary and job description:

Bavasi probably makes about $55,000 a year. He supervises all player matters (salary negotiations, trades, roster cutdowns, minor league player assignments, free-agent signings) and handles miscellaneous paper work. Of course, much of the actual work is done by his staff, whose counsel he seeks on all important matters. "It's enough to keep a man busy eight hours a day," Buzzie said. "But the hard part of the job is the tension, not the work. In baseball, you have to win. In other businesses, a lot of companies may have great years all at once, but in our league, there is only one winner."

In the twenty-first century a corporate mentality forces many GMs to divide their time among dealing with agents, negotiating contracts, and tracking the bottom line. But for GMs of Buzzie Bavasi's era the most critical part of the job was evaluating talent. Acquiring the right players to build a winning team—and staying within an owner's budget while doing so—required a scout's eye and a manager's Olympian view of what a team needed. Late in his life Buzzie recorded some advice for fans on how to watch a baseball game. It reflects his deep knowledge of player evaluations. He made notes on each position. For a first baseman the notes read as follows:

This is the easiest position to scout.

A) Should usually have some power. Does your first baseman have power to all fields?

B) Can he make the play to second base on an attempted bunt[?] If he can, then it determines two things for you: His arm is above average and he has some agility.

C) Has your first baseman been converted from another position? Many of the good ones were . . . Steve Garvey, Rod Carew, Pete Rose, Gil Hodges and many other[s].

D) Beware of the first baseman who leads his league in fielding average. This usually means he isn't doing his job. What it is telling us is that when a ground ball is hit to right field, the first baseman is moving nothing but his eyeballs.

For the shortstop, Bavasi's notes were as follows:

A) I doubt you've ever seen a winning club without a good short-stop. He is the glue that keeps an infield together.

B) The arm is important. Does your man have a good arm or does he get the ball away quickly, ala Leo Durocher who had a medio-cre arm, but got the ball to first in a hurry[?]

C) Watch to see where he plays the hitter. A good shortstop is a groundskeeper's delight. Never stays in one spot long enough to kill the grass.

D) Does your shortstop pick up on the type of pitch being thrown and does he pass this information on to his teammates[?]

His notes about the catcher end on a poignant memory:

A) Is he in charge of the game?

B) Is he calling the pitches or is he getting signs from the bench?

C) Is he alert and agile[?] Does he anticipate the opponents' next move?

D) Count the number of balls he drops. Particularly with a man on first base.

E) Try to catch with him. Call the pitch for him. Curve, fastball, slider, etc.

F) I'm not being fair, but I compare all catchers with Roy Cam-panella.

Such notes all speak to Bavasi's ability to see the specific gifts that a player would need to make a contribution to a team. Per-haps foremost was his knack for identifying the bottom-of-the-roster players who become the essential bits of mortar that hold a club together. Buzzie's son Bill Bavasi, a long-time GM him-self, calls the bottom-of-the-roster players "Einsteins in their field." It is much harder for a player to have success when he is not playing every game but rather is making spot appearances and is expected to produce. It is the Al Ferraras that make the difference between a championship and a second-place team, and Buzzie Bavasi treasured them. The fact that Ferrara was an endless source of inspiration to his teammates—always encouraging, positive, their biggest booster even when he was sitting on the bench—is one of those intangible assets that a good GM values. The Bull's high spirits, which carried him through life on and off the field, lifted an entire team up. Ferrara was also someone who never feared life. He sought out challenges, off and on the field, and never backed down. That was an intangible character trait that Buzzie Bavasi knew was part of a winning team.

Bavasi's comments about pitchers spoke directly to his philosophy of finding players with courage:

A) I guess all of us can tell when a pitcher can throw a ball 90 miles an hour, but to know when he is going to throw it is the important thing.

B) Does he challenge hitters?

C) Watch a pitcher for an inning or two and then try to detect what pitch he is throwing.

D) Watch his feet, watch his arm extension, watch to see if he throws pitches in sequence.

E) Pitching is the backbone of the game, but also the one position that takes many things into consideration. 1. Determination. 2. Concentration. 3. Intestinal fortitude (even more so than the regular player). I remember Roger Craig in 1959 when he pitched for the Dodgers. During that year when he won 11 and lost 5, Roger was in such pain that tears would come to his eyes on every pitch, but he never gave up. Imagine pitching a no-hitter with an arthritic left shoulder. . . . Well, Sandy Koufax did it twice.

It was pitching, defense, and speed that marked the 1963 Dodgers as perhaps one of the best Dodger teams ever. After they won the 1963 world championship, Bavasi wanted to overtake the Yankees as baseball's preeminent dynasty. Then came the miserable 1964 season. Such a season wasn't supposed to happen to this team. Bavasi knew he had to do something. His plan started that winter.

Bavasi had more good outfielders than he could use, and one of them was the giant power hitter Frank Howard. In the spring of 1964 Howard had received permission to miss the first two weeks at Vero Beach to resolve "personal problems." Dodger historian Mark Langill wrote that Howard had sent a handwritten letter to Bavasi letting him know he was going to retire from baseball at the age of twenty-seven: "Physically and mentally, I do not feel like playing. I would be no good to the team or to myself. It is with deep regret I am quitting baseball, but I have made up my mind." Howard did not retire. Buzzie talked him into playing, but Howard's gentle and humble demeanor, as appealing as it was in other walks of life, was not the kind of steely nerve that Bavasi was looking for.

On December 4, 1964, Bavasi traded Howard, strong enough to hit home runs out of pitcher-friendly Dodger Stadium, to the Washington Senators. Seven players were involved, but the crucial Senator coming to the Dodgers was pitcher Claude Osteen. Bavasi had met with manager Walter Alston and all the coaches, and they agreed that with or without Frank Howard, the team didn't have enough offense. The solution? Get better pitching. It was classic Bavasi thinking, a creative solution that addressed the problem from a different side. Bavasi himself gave credit for the Osteen trade to veteran scout Ted McGrew. At the time, McGrew was in his eighties and semi-retired, but each summer Buzzie paid his expenses for a hotel room in Chicago, and McGrew would watch either the Cubs or White Sox play. When McGrew heard that Buzzie was looking for a good left-handed pitcher, he called and said, "Osteen's your man." But most important, they had found someone in the Bavasi mold—a man with ice in his veins.

That December Al "the Bull" Ferrara was playing winter league ball in the Dominican Republic. He had been on the world championship Dodger team in 1963 but had spent the whole of 1964 back at the AAA Minor League team in Spokane. He was relishing life in the Dominican Republic. He was confident that he would become an everyday player for the Dodgers, and he was having a strong season in Santo Domingo. He was staying at the Ambassador Hotel (where he discovered the manicurist would make room visits for daily services) and hitting over .300. "If you hit really good in this country, they treat you like you're the king," he concluded. He had a personal driver, Mauesto, who was a cousin to the fabled baseball Alou brothers. The personal driver wasn't really a luxury; as a native New Yorker, the Bull had never learned how to drive a car. One day Mauesto said his mother would like to meet Ferrara. The Bull was always open to meeting new people, and they hopped in the car. Mauesto drove them out of the city, along the winding roads that led deep into the jungle. Finally, on an unpaved road carved between trees, in the middle of the wilderness, they came to a solitary hut. Mauesto led them inside to a dirt floor and a space illuminated by candles. Mauesto's mother sat on the ground beside an immense pot. The Bull looked into the bubbling pot, and Mauesto explained, "Ferrara, you know what this is? *Chivo guisado picante*—spicy goat stew."

"He thought I wouldn't like it," the Bull mused. "But in my childhood in Brooklyn, my father took me to Avenue U, and we ate sheepshead and intestine. I was happy to eat this—in the hut, with the candles." Ferrara had a knack for embracing people based on their character rather than their circumstances. Ferrara made dinner with Mauesto and his mother a Sunday ritual that resonated with his childhood memories.

Like the intensity of those playing stickball games in the streets without gloves, the Dominicans were full of a passionate intensity for the game of baseball. The games were wondrous, colorful events, with fans parading through the stands in dragon costumes. In one game Ferrara bumped an umpire by accident during an argument and was suspended for a game. Following batting practice the next day, he got into his street clothes and watched from the stands. Fans flocked to him; they appreciated that an American had come there to play hard and well.

Of course being Al Ferrara, he played hard and well off the field too. Nightclubs in the Dominican Republic were essentially bars with bands and tables. One night he got into a "half-baked brawl with a guy." The police put the fighters into a paddy wagon, and the Bull's opponent asked who he was. "Al Ferrara." It turned out the brawler was the brother of the great San Francisco Giants pitcher Juan Marichal. The future Hall of Famer came to the police station and bailed them both out.

Ferrara made an art out of living life on the edge. Whether it was eating goat stew in a hut in the jungle or frequenting the night clubs of Santo Domingo, he found joy in pushing the boundaries of convention. Such a stance doesn't necessarily mean outrageous behavior; sometimes it means a willingness to go where others fear to tread. As Al said, "I loved eating that goat stew in the jungle. I didn't get drunk—just had a great day with a guy who wanted me to meet his mother. Where are you going to beat that—a place where people really give a damn about you?"

The Bull's poignant question encapsulates his lifetime search, expressed with his outsized conviviality, for a place where people truly cared about each other. The defining moment of his life occurred when he was nineteen. He came home and discovered an ambulance taking his mother to the hospital. She had suffered the second stroke of her relatively young life. At three that morning, his father got a phone call from the hospital—his mother, who had held the family together—was dead. Who else truly cared about Al Ferrara Jr.? In the land of baseball, where players come and go and get demoted or traded to distant cities at the drop of a hat, where indeed could a man find a place where people truly cared about *him* and the heart that beat under his jersey?

When the Bull returned to North America from Santo Domingo in January 1965, he was ready for spring training. He was convinced the Frank Howard trade had opened up an outfield spot, and he could be the power hitter to replace Howard. He had been on the 1963 world championship team, and it was only the surfeit of superb outfielders in 1964 that had kept him in the Minor Leagues that year. But now his season would come. He was sure that he would come to spring training competing for the right field job with young left-handed-hitting Derrell Griffith. Ferrara was confident that this would be his time to play every day, to break out, and to fulfill his destiny. In February 1965 the Bull reported to Vero Beach with the highest of hopes. But in baseball, as in life, man plans—and God laughs.

Spring Training   **2**

February and March are the most gracious of baseball months. They unfold in lazy towns in Florida and Arizona; the games have the intimate feel of town ball contests, in which the spectators grab a beer with the shortstops after the game. It's a world apart from the regular season, and the venues have an identity completely separate from the big ball parks in the Majors. A baseball team's spring training facility doesn't reflect its home ball park—except for Dodgertown.

No facility captured the gestalt of its hometown like Dodgertown did in the 1950s and '60s. The Dodgers proudly broke baseball's color line in 1947, and Dodgertown's very reason for being was tied to its groundbreaking civil rights history. In the winter of 1946 Buzzie Bavasi had been dispatched by Branch Rickey, then president, general manager, and part owner of the Dodgers, to find a place in Florida where Jackie Robinson and the entire Dodger team could live, eat, and play out of the shadow of Jim Crow. Bavasi was shown Vero Beach and didn't look anywhere else. Because they needed a self-contained island of integration within the segregated South, the Dodgers created a baseball enclave in the Florida wetlands, complete with multiple fields, pool tables, and a golf course. The town and the Dodgers arrived at a trade-off to achieve this: local segregation laws were not enforced within Dodgertown, but when exhibition games were played at Holman Field, Jim Crow prevailed. There were separate entrances, restrooms, water fountains, and seating for white and black spectators in the stadium. In truth calling it "seating" for black patrons was a linguistic stretch; Al Ferrara remembers his shock at seeing black fans sitting on the grass behind right field.

While the Los Angeles Dodgers of the early 1960s were the toast of Hollywood, Dodgertown still echoed Flatbush. The eccentric backstage personnel in Vero Beach remained the same as they had been a decade earlier. Men with vague job descriptions at best—like Herman Levy or the eccentric fellow known as "Beansy"—were ever present, Runyonesque characters who tagged along with the gang performing odd jobs. Beansy, for example, was a ghostly pale man who might have been a plumber but primarily ran horse-racing wagers to the track on behalf of the team.

"Beansy was the whitest guy you ever saw—like the blood had been drained out of him," Ferrara remembers. "Everybody was drinking; drinking was the thing. Beansy would walk straight through a crowd, like an atmosphere guy in the movies, and he was deathly pale, and we'd go, 'Please, Beansy, don't take another drink.'"

One day, having collected the wagers from the team, Beansy was walking through the Dodgertown grounds. He suddenly stopped, turned a more luminous shade of white, collapsed like a sniper had gunned him down, and died of a heart attack. As he lay on the ground, in their best Brooklyn fashion, players sent somebody over to retrieve their money. There is indeed no crying in baseball.

The cast of characters included a medical team of sorts. John "Doc" Mattei was the team trainer, a podiatrist from Cleveland players called the Penguin. A short man who wobbled when he walked, he talked out of the side of his mouth through an ever-present cigar. Although his medical background was in podiatry, he tended to medical needs well above the foot. Much of his job involved handing out doses of penicillin; venereal disease was an occupational hazard. The resident infirmary nurse, possessed of the Dickensian name of Anastasia Plucker, was dressed completely in white, with a starched white hat perched on her head. The Bull recalls, "You'd go to her if you didn't feel so good, and she'd give you these pills that would change the texture of your urine. She was very dedicated."

Mail delivery to the six hundred players was handled by the eccentric flag-raiser Herman Levy. Every morning Levy, who had a photographic memory, could recall precisely which of the hundreds of players had received letters. At the end of one spring training Levy found that Mrs. O'Malley had left a lamp behind at Vero Beach. He rode a Greyhound bus across the United States, arrived in Los Angeles, took a taxi to Dodger Stadium, brought the lamp up to Buzzie Bavasi's office, and said, "Mrs. O'Malley left this." Then he got back in the taxi and took the bus back to Florida.

Bavasi and the O'Malley family had a fondness for these *Guys and Dolls* characters. They represented a nostalgic thread back to Ebbets Field, and it would be another generation before the Brooklyn roots finally withered away and the Dodgers personnel became strictly Californian. Into the mid-1960s Dodger Stadium in Los Angeles felt like Flatbush West. Indeed the cultural mix of East Coast and West Coast was apparent even in the way players danced. There was a jukebox in the lobby of the barracks in Vero Beach, and players would get up and dance. "You could see the difference," says Ferrara. "East Coast guys were doing Chubby Checker, and then Willie Davis [who went to high school in Los Angeles] would get up and be doing a different thing." Players naturally brought the worlds with which they were familiar to Vero Beach. The Bull and a hard-throwing pitching prospect from Brooklyn named Carmine Chercella hung out together. (Dodger scout—later to become manager—Tommy Lasorda explained Chercella's problem as a pitcher: "Carmine could throw a ball through a brick wall. The only thing is, he can't hit the damn wall.") The Bull and Carmine were used to hanging out on Brooklyn street corners near drugstores, which were kind of informal community gathering places. So they emulated that behavior in Vero Beach. They found a drugstore in the tiny sunny town and loitered at a moribund corner. Dodger vice-president Fresco Thompson called them "drugstore cowboys."

At the beginning of each spring training Thompson gave the newcomers an orientation. In the world of 1950s baseball a vice-president was not a man in a gray flannel suit, but in Thompson's case he was a tough old ballplayer who had played mainly with the Phillies. He was a needler, that baseball type who found joy in endlessly teasing his fellow travelers in the baseball world. When a player asked for a raise because he had a new baby and thus an additional mouth to feed, Thompson's standard reply was, "We pay you for your ability, not your fertility."

Fresco's orientation message was this: "We're here to judge you. We want to give you a chance. If your arm is sore, instead of wearing a blue Dodger cap, wear a white one. If your leg is sore, instead of wearing a blue Dodger stocking, wear a white one so that the scout knows you have a bad leg." Ferrara remembered playing catch with a guy wearing a white hat. Two days later that player was gone. The next day he played catch with someone wearing white socks. The day after that, that player was gone. The Bull quickly came to a conclusion: "I'm not wearing white. Anybody injured was going home."

All around the camp the Dodgers had placed jugs of grapefruit juice. The players were encouraged to drink it; they were told it was the best thing for them. Fresco Thompson would insist that if they drank the grapefruit juice, they'd go to the big leagues. Years later Ferrara found out why the team pushed the grapefruit juice: it was loaded with saltpeter, which dampens the libido. "They wanted us to—how shall I say it?—concentrate on baseball," he said.

The Minor League players lived in barracks, four to a room, in double bunks, with no air conditioning. There was a strict 11 p.m. curfew, which, of course, the Bull immediately ignored. His attitude throughout his playing career was that he gave his team 100 percent on the field. What he did with his own time was his business.

In Vero Beach Major Leaguers and coaches drank at Lenny's "New" Bar; Minor Leaguers went to Lenny's "Old." The Bull was a regular at Lenny's Old, which meant he routinely found him-

self scaling the big fence around Dodgertown long after curfew. The team locked the barracks door, but a helpful teammate
would leave a window open. Scouts patrolled the grounds with
flashlights, like amateur prison guards searching for a jail break.
One night Al was coming over the fence and a flashlight hit him.
He ran; his pursuer chased him and caught him. Al reports: "He
shines the light on my face and says what the hell are you doing
out? I said I fell asleep with a girl. He says, 'Do you know they
could send you home? What's your name?' 'Al Ferrara.' 'You're
Italian.' 'Yeah.'"

The scout was Tommy Lasorda. Al continues: "[Lasorda said,]
'I'm not going to turn in an Italian guy. But if I ever catch you
again, you're going home.' And he helps me up through the window." During the season Lasorda got his payback: he endlessly
enlisted the Bull to come with him to speak to Rotary Clubs,
Kiwanis Clubs, and at schools. The Bull almost wished Lasorda
had turned him in.

The Bull's first spring training had been in 1959. He was Brooklyn born and bred and had come to the Dodgers' attention at an
Ebbets Field tryout, where he had tagged along with a friend to
shag fly balls. In his senior year in high school he was mired in a
horrible slump and batted just .083. But somehow he remained
convinced he could play Major League baseball. When he got
his chance to bat at the tryout, he hit the ball out of the park in
his first three swings. The Dodgers grabbed him, and two years
later the Bull was headed to his first spring training. He flew to
Florida on the "ко" prop jet—named for the owner's wife, Kay
O'Malley. His father and his uncle Joe took him to the hanger,
where Uncle Joe left him with a piece of sage advice: "Keep it in
your pants." The Bull says of that moment, "At that time it wasn't
a big deal. Turned out to be a big deal later."

On his first day of the 1959 spring training, the Bull sat down
to eat and realized he was sitting next to Major Leaguer Jim Gilliam. Here was a player he had watched from the stands—he
had cheered for him, been a fan of his—and now he was sitting
next to him as a fellow Dodger. That was by design—a design

directed by Buzzie Bavasi. Within Dodgertown the Dodgers were one large family. All six hundred players intermingled. So when a rookie came up to the big leagues, as the Bull did in 1963, he already knew the players. The gap between Minor League prospect and Major League player was not an impossible leap but a step up to a group of men who already knew each other. Likewise, the tradition of how to play Dodger baseball was passed on in a deeply personal way. The wisdom of Pee Wee Reese and Roy Campanella still hovered around the players, informing how they approached the game. Ferrara remembers two lasting aphorisms from the "Boys of Summer"—that is, the Brooklyn Dodgers—that informed the Dodgers of the 1960s: "If you rush in and out of the clubhouse, you will rush in and out of baseball." It was important to spend time with each other, to be a good teammate. And: "If you don't show up to play, then take your uniform off and give it to someone who wants to play." Dodgertown, planted in a tiny Florida town, replete with snakes and cockroaches, set in an old military barracks, bonded players across baseball's hierarchy.

Al came face to face with this phenomenon during his first spring training. He stepped in to bat during a practice game, looked out, and saw that he was going to face Johnny Podres. Podres was a superb left-handed pitcher, a big game pitcher par excellence, an epitome of Bavasi's goal of a player with nerves of steel. He was the hero of the 1955 World Series, winning Game Seven. He was the man who finally defeated the Yankees and brought a championship to Brooklyn. Pod could walk into any bar in Brooklyn (and frequently did so); the bartender would announce that Johnny Podres was in the house, and within minutes the bar would be full of fans, all clamoring to buy him a drink. Now, four years after a teenage Al Ferrara had cheered Podres from the stands, the Bull was in the batter's box, facing him.

Suddenly Buzzie Bavasi ran down to the field. The Bull remembers: "Buzzie loved Podres. Buzzie yells, 'Anybody gets a hit off him gets twenty bucks.' I got into the box; he threw a change up—which was his great pitch—and I lined one down the left-field line and got a double. Buzzie comes running over with a twenty dollar bill. Podres was probably hung over. He was glaring at me."

It was a memorable way to meet Buzzie Bavasi. Since the free agency era a wall has gone up between players and management; they are in opposition much of the time over contracts and negotiations. In the multi-billion-dollar business of today's baseball the players provide the core entertainment value—they are the product—and management's job is to make money for the owners. While this was also true in Buzzie's era, the teams were owned by individuals. The modern corporate structure of baseball ownership has embedded a distance between management and talent; separating owner and employee is now professional sports' strongest union. The notion of Buzzie racing onto the diamond with a twenty-dollar bill for a young guy who had just gotten a hit off his hero is inconceivable today for many reasons: a GM would never run onto the field like that; he would never risk offending one of his star pitchers; and, most important, the personal relationship between management and players has changed. The ability to joke freely, which is always the mark of real understanding between two people, no longer exists.

There's an inherent tension during spring training among players fighting to get on the roster. A player wants to be a good teammate, but he is also competing with those teammates for a job. Ron Fairly recalls how this tension played out in his first spring training. During batting practice he asked manager Walter Alston where he wanted him to go. Alston told him to go to right field, and there stood Carl Furillo. Furillo was one of the Boys of Summer who perennially stood in front of the Abe Stark "HIT SIGN, WIN SUIT" billboard on the lower portion of the hand-operated scoreboard at Ebbets Field.

Years later, Buzzie's son Bob was building a replica of this famous scoreboard for his Minor League team's ballpark in Everett, Washington, right down to the "HIT SIGN, WIN SUIT" billboard. While Bob was hustling a potential sponsor for that billboard, the man reasonably asked, "How many suits am I going to give away?" Bob said, "Let's call the general manager of the Brooklyn Dodgers right now." Buzzie answered the fellow: "Carl Furillo was my right fielder and we didn't give away any, but I don't know who Bob's got." The man chuckled and signed.

Now rookie Ron Fairly approached the storied veteran and introduced himself. Furillo replied, "Nice to meet you. I am the right fielder on this team, and you can have it when I'm finished with it. I'm not finished yet." But every veteran of that era knew that his livelihood depended on the strength of his teammates—the World Series share could make or break a player's financial year. As Furillo said to his teammates when he was sitting out a day, "Fellas, you're playing with my money today. Do something with it." So finding a player who busted his ass every time he was on the field was a happy occasion. All the veterans on the Dodgers agreed that Al Ferrara was that kind of player. As Fairly said years later about Ferrara's intensity and commitment to the team, "And, you know, there's no stat for that."

Johnny Podres and the Bull quickly became best friends. When Ferrara played his first Major League season in 1963, they were linchpins of the Mayfair Mafia, a never-ending party at the Mayfair Hotel in downtown Los Angeles. Now it was 1965. Buzzie Bavasi was convinced his club had a shot at winning the World Series and cementing a legacy as the dominant team of its time. Corralling the behavior of Podres and the Bull was vital to his plan for success. In his typically imaginative way of problem solving, Bavasi decided upon a social engineering experiment. Buzzie called the two rounders into his office and told them he was putting them together as roommates. His strategic thinking was that troublemakers might as well be placed together instead of planting separate fuses in the barracks, which might ignite other players. Buzzie told them, "I think you fellows are going to be prominent this year. I'm asking you to cool it. Do not go out and get drunk every night."

The Bull replied, "Buzzie, tell you what I'm going to do. I brought my record player, and me and John can listen to music in the room all night." Half a century later the Bull recalls: "So we go to the room the first night and put on the record player, and within ten minutes I'm thinking, this ain't going to happen." Ferrara loaded the record player with a stack of records that would play throughout the evening, so people would assume he and Podres were in the room. They went out and returned at two in the morning. "The record player had got stuck, and the same record had been playing over and over for five hours."

The next morning Buzzie came storming down the aisle of the barracks, saying, "You two dumb bunnies kept Wes Parker and half the barracks up with your music." Podres told Buzzie, "It wasn't us." "What do you mean?" Buzzie replied. "Ferrara's got a record player." "Yeah," said Podres with a straight face, "but we were out all night."

Bavasi had the Sisyphean task of continuously monitoring the duo he had put together. Podres had a fondness for pigs feet. He purchased immense jars of pigs feet with pickles. In the heat of a Vero Beach un-air-conditioned room, the smell was hideous. So Bavasi had to lay down the law about odor as well as sound: "Podres, get rid of those pigs feet."

One morning a workout was canceled because of rain. Podres, who shared a love of horse racing with the Bull, begged Ferrara to ride with him to the Gulfstream racetrack. But it was four hours away, so it didn't seem possible. Then teammate Don Miles heard them talking about it. Miles had played in Victoria, Texas, where he had fallen in love with the wealthy owner's daughter and married her. Her father had a small private plane, and Miles had flown it to Vero Beach. He heard Podres and the Bull talking and said, "I'll fly you to Gulfstream Park. Let's go."

The three went to the Vero Beach airport, hopped in Miles's plane, and flew to Miami. They took a cab to the racetrack, played the horses, and, of course, drank at the bar. In the cab on the way back to the Miami airport Podres suggested to Miles that they stop en route in West Palm Beach and take in some dog racing. Miles was enthusiastic about the idea, so the three flew to the West Palm Beach dog track. More drinking ensued. At eleven o'clock at night they took off from West Palm Beach for the short hop to Vero Beach. Don Miles's plane got over Vero Beach's small airport at midnight, and the crew there didn't want to give him clearance to land. It was foggy, it was past the airport's official closing hour; there was no way the crew could allow this plane to land. Miles objected: "I've got Al Ferrara and Johnny Podres in this plane." Finally the tower made an exception, and Miles brought the plane down safely.

Ferrara remembers that news of this adventure spread all over camp, and the next day Buzzie walked into the clubhouse, steaming with anger: "Did you know O'Malley is going crazy? There's no insurance for you fellows in a private airplane. What are you trying to do?" The Bull replied, "All we were trying to do is make a bet. There were no women involved, no fights—what more do you want?"

What more could Buzzie Bavasi want? In the spring of 1965 he wanted another championship team. As camp broke, he was excited about the team's chances. The pitching had improved with the acquisition of Osteen. The defense was much better with the addition of young infielders John Kennedy, who had come over in the Osteen trade, and Jim Lefebvre. In 1964 a rookie named Wes Parker had started playing first base. He would turn out to be perhaps the finest defensive first baseman of the decade, if not one of the best of all time. Wes Parker had pushed Ron Fairly into the outfield. Now the Dodgers had a superb defensive infield to support their starting pitching, which was the best in baseball. There was no reason why they couldn't win it all. During spring training Ferrara had hit well. Derrell Griffith had faded, and it seemed clear that manager Walter Alston had a platoon system in mind in right field: the final two weeks of spring training Ron Fairly would start against a right-handed pitcher, and Ferrara would start against a lefty. The Bull had his chance.

As the Dodgers left Vero Beach, in the best spring training fashion, everyone's sky was blue: the Dodgers had improved their pitching and fielding, the Bull was confident there was a place for him in the outfield, and Buzzie Bavasi was aiming for another world championship.

April 3

The Bull leans forward on a chair in his Studio City apartment. It is 2015, fifty years after the most tumultuous season of his life. He comments: "Alston was one of them guys that walked around very drably dressed. He had a fedora hat on, and he didn't drink." He's speaking of Walter Alston, manager of the Brooklyn Dodgers in their championship decade of the 1950s and then the Los Angeles Dodgers during the glory days of the 1960s. Alston was the man in whom Buzzie Bavasi put his faith through twenty-four consecutive one-year contracts. The Bull continues: "Alston would call team meetings, and he always used to start off with: 'You're nothing but a bunch of whiskey-drinking, skirt-chasing assholes.' Then his hand would shake, and he would get a cigarette. His nickname was 'Smokey' because he smoked like a chimney. His hand would shake, and then you knew that he was gonna get to the real reason for the meeting: somebody screwed up, somebody did this or that." Much of the time in 1965 that somebody was Al "the Bull" Ferrara. He never stopped having a good time.

On Opening Day 1965 Ferrara was living a lifelong dream: he was a Los Angeles Dodger. Ferrara's habitual apparel remains a Dodger T-shirt and a Dodger windbreaker. His glasses are tinted Dodger blue. Baseball has been the love of his life, and the Dodgers are his longest relationship. He miraculously played for the team he grew up adoring, moving with them when they landed on the other side of the country. Now in his mid-seventies, he retains a Brooklyn accent and unique vocabulary. The Bull is built for power:

large shoulders, a barrel chest. When he picks up a bat to illustrate how he adjusted his stance after getting advice from fellow Minor Leaguer Jay Ward, it is easy to imagine the explosive power of his swing forty years after he last stood in a batter's box. Like all professional athletes, he's at home in his body; the bat becomes an effortless extension of his body, and its weight seems to disappear.

For a moment it seems he will actually swing the bat in his dining room, sending a laptop perched on the table flying into the gap. But he is just demonstrating his grip. In the Minor Leagues he started lifting his pointer finger completely off the bat, and that became a characteristic stance one sees in every baseball card photo of Ferrara. He puts the bat down and brushes his hands, as if wiping off dirt, saying, "Never changed that [stance] my whole career. People saw those cards and thought I was giving the finger, but that's just the way I held the bat." Actors speak of finding a defining character gesture. For the Bull it is this brushing of the hands. That gesture—"Okay, I've done that, and it's behind me"—is a physicalization of a remarkable ability to live in the moment. It is the universal baseball sign for "That batter got a hit; okay, I'm moving on to the next pitch" or "Lost that game; let's move on to the next game" or "That season is finished; we're moving on to next season." There's always a next season in Al Ferrara's life. But there will never be another season like the summer of '65.

The season opened on April 14 with a game against the Mets in New York. The Bull was in his hometown; his friends and family were at the game. The final week of spring training had continued to unfold as anticipated. Tommy Davis was the left fielder; he was a superstar, a two-time batting champion, at the height of his career. Willie Davis was the center fielder, an excellent defensive player and a speed demon. And in right field, as had been the case through spring training, Ron Fairly started against right-handed pitchers and Ferrara started against lefties. The Opening Day pitcher for the Mets was Alvin Jackson—a leftie. Ferrara arrived at Shea Stadium, which had just opened the year before. He looked at the lineup card. Starting in right field: Ron Fairly. The Bull was disappointed but didn't show his frustration. This was just the first game of the year; baseball stretches out over a long season. And he did get into the game, playing an inning in the outfield. The season was new; surely his time was coming.

It was April; there was rain, and the second game of the season wasn't played until Saturday, April 17. Ferrara pinch-hit late in the game and grounded out. He didn't play the next day. The Dodgers flew back to Los Angeles for their home opener on Tuesday, April 20. They faced the aging Hall of Fame left-hander Warren Spahn, who was pitching for the Mets at the end of his career. Although a left-handed pitcher was on the mound, once again Ron Fairly started in right. The Bull pinch-hit late in the game and rocketed a triple off of Spahn. That felt auspicious; it should mean good things were to come. But Ferrara didn't play in the next five games. Sitting on the bench, Ferrara pondered the long road that had taken him from Brooklyn to Dodger Stadium.

When Alfred Ferrara Jr. was born on December 22, 1939, the population of Brooklyn was 2,695,000. On its own it would have been America's third-largest city, yet it had the feel of a small town. Neighbors knew each other; kids played punchball in the street; mom-and-pop shops were on every corner. It was intimate. Manhattan was an island of concrete canyons; Brooklyn was a cluster of brownstones. The Bronx had the colossus of Yankee Stadium; Brooklyn claimed Ebbets Field. New York—which to the world at large meant Manhattan—was the epicenter of sophistication. Brooklyn was mocked as the home of "dese, dems, and dose." In 1941 Brooklynite Sidney H. Ascher formed the Society to Prevent Disparaging Remarks about Brooklyn, hoping to staunch the image of the Brooklyn resident as unlettered. Brooklyn played the beloved underdog, and its team embodied the blue-collar character of the borough. Manhattan was the place where a parent went to work in an office building and the sidewalks were crowded with adults hurrying to work or shop. Brooklyn's streets were crowded with kids playing potsy and double-dutch jump rope and zipping down sidewalks on scooters they had made by nailing roller skates to a pear box. Manhat-

tan was home to fine restaurants; in Brooklyn the favorite foods
were a half-sour pickle out of a barrel, skinny pretzels, and malted
milks. The neighborhood cop knew every child on the block, and
in the summer all the windows were open and radios could be
heard up and down the streets. The smell of boiling tomatoes
filled the air along with the sound of Red Barber's play-by-play.

In 1939 a second world war was still a distant thought, though
on the horizon, and the Great Depression was slowly lifting. The
Brooklyn Dodgers had just come off a promising season, led by
their new manager and shortstop, Leo Durocher. The Dodgers
had passed through their "Daffiness Boys" era, epitomized when
visiting player Casey Stengel came to home plate, doffed his hat,
and a sparrow flew out. Going into spring training of 1939, fans
hoped that the Dodgers might win the pennant for the first time
since 1920, when they were still known as the Brooklyn Robins.
Al Ferrara Jr. grew up in this Brooklyn idyll, recounted in count-
less memoirs, where everywhere the talk was of baseball.

The Bull's Italian parents represented a split personality. His
father, Alfred Ferrara Sr., was stern, a somber and penurious
immigrant who watched every penny. His mother, Adelle—"Delia"
or "Del"—grew up in the Paulucci family, who were affectionate
bon vivants. They would gather at Delia's invitation every Sunday afternoon: Uncle Oscar Paulucci, a prize fighter who went
by the name of "Mickey Paul"; Aunt Edna, a hand walker who
into middle age could walk along a tree branch on her hands;
the cousins and brothers and sisters. They would drink and tell
stories and laugh and argue, and eventually each Sunday someone would storm off in a fury of alcohol and familial anger. Delia
would spend the week patching up the family relationships, invite
them all over again, and the cycle would repeat.

There was just one bedroom in the Ferrara apartment at 1431
East Second Street, where five people slept: the two parents in one
bed and the three children crowded into a bunk bed, Al sleeping
on the top bunk while the young twins shared the bunk below.
Ferrara remembers that when the suffocating heat of summer
filled up the one bedroom, he would take a pillow and sleep on the

fire escape. He'd look down at the street below him, which was his baseball field. This was his first home field, a beloved ballpark improvised out of a Brooklyn street. A car served as first base, a manhole cover was second base, and another car was third. If a player hit a ball two sewers, he was really something. Right by third base, in an apartment building, lived a little blonde girl with curls named Patty who had contracted polio. She was in an iron lung in the house. Between innings Al would call up to her from the field: "Hi, Patty; how ya doin'?" Like all the innocence of Brooklyn in the 1950s, Patty had passed away by 1965.

The Ferrara apartment was on the fourth floor, and the Bull's grandmother Asunta lived on the first floor. The family called her "Sue," but Al gave her the name "Othermama," and her grandchildren called her that the rest of her life. Her apartment was larger than the one upstairs, and Al's great-grandmother Lena lived there with her. Ferrara remembers that Lena "had solid white hair. She was very, very old. Among the family, in my earliest recollections, when they talked about Lena, I would hear the word 'crazy.' She was crazy. To me she was not so crazy. She was my shadow; she was all over me."

At the end of the Ferrara's block was a bus line that ran through Brooklyn to Shore Parkway. At the age of four Al insisted that Lena take him on the bus. "I loved to be on that bus," he recalls. "Lena would sit me by the window, and she sat on the side. We got to the end, we'd get off, and we'd take the bus back. We'd do it two or three times a day."

Then one day Lena died. Al remembers: "The casket was in the house, in the room closest to the window in my grandmother's apartment. Lena was laid out in the casket. It was my first casket, and I kneeled at that coffin almost all the time for three days, hoping she would wake up. Every once in a while I swore she moved. I ran into Mom and told her. My mother looked at me and shook her head. I really learned how to cry when they took her away. I never rode the buses again."

Ferrara has a vivid memory of the day in 1945 when the war ended: "We had a block party. We set up tables outside, full of food.

It was an Italian block party to welcome back kids from the war. I had three uncles coming back I had never met." One of them was his mother's brother Harold, a terrific baseball player who got a scholarship to St. John's. Another was Oscar Paulucci. "He was always showing up in the neighborhood driving a big convertible, squiring good-looking women," the Bull recalls. "He married a Jewish girl by the name of Molly and bought a bar. Uncle Oscar with the big car was the high roller; whatever you did, he went around the corner and straightened it out."

All summer Al and his friends, like Bobby Wiese and David Gutfeld and "Fly-Shit-on-Nose" (because he had a small mole on his nose), would play stickball and punchball, dodging cars and even horse manure when the watermelon man would park his wagon in the street and deliver melons. Ferrara's eyes light up as he remembers the street in front of his apartment: "That's where I learned [how to play ball]. Once you had breakfast, you'd get out of the house and go down to the field. The street would be divided into big boys and little boys, and you'd figure out a ballgame. The street brought me wonderful joy—I loved it. Every day I'd take my broomstick down to the street—that was my bat. Stickball was played with a Spaldeen."

(The Spalding Company manufactured a small red rubber ball, technically named the Spalding Hi-Bounce Ball, which became a foundation of stickball and punchball. New Yorkers pronounced it "Spaldeen," and eventually the company took out a trademark on that spelling and used it in its marketing. Ferrara remembers, "You'd have a Spaldeen, and if it went down the sewer, you had to fish it out. Past the sewer, that was second base. There was a tree that grew, a big tree, and its branches covered the field. Balls went into that tree. There were no hitting coaches. No mentors. I'd get a newspaper with a picture of someone hitting and go up to the roof and try to emulate that swing. I saw a picture of Ted Williams, and I'd tried to copy him.")

The games were serious competitions. When Second Street played Third Street, neighbors would come out and sit in beach chairs to watch. If there weren't enough guys to play a game that day, Al would go next door, where there was an open lot covered with weeds. He describes playing in the lot: "All weeds and rocks, too narrow to play a game. But I'd take my stickball bat and pick up a rock and throw it in the air. I'd hit rocks. I'd be Stan Musial; I'd be Joe DiMaggio. One day I hit a rock that went all the way to Third Street. Another broken window on Third Street."

Ferrara attended St. Athanasius grade school and played his first organized baseball there on a field that had no grass and was loaded with rocks. So both of his childhood home fields were hard-scrabble. The teachers at St. Athanasius were all nuns. "Tough Irish women," Al says. "They'd whack you with a ruler. In seventh grade I had Sister Georgina. She was a participant in this ruler stuff—I was getting whacked all the time." One day she assigned the class to write an essay on the topic "What do you want to be when you grow up?" Al wrote that he wanted to be a baseball player. He read his essay, and Sister Georgina pulled his ear and told him to put his hand out: whack! Al asked her what he had done wrong, and she replied, "You've got to get reasonable. Get your priorities straight." In 1963, Al's first year in the big leagues, he played against the Mets in the Polo Grounds. Before the game he came out on the field to warm up and heard a voice call, "Alfred." He looked up. At the edge of the dugout, wearing the same black habit, was Sister Georgina. He walked up to her, and she hugged him and said, "I'm so proud of you." And she cried.

In 1947 Ferrara attended his first Major League baseball game. The man who took him was the coach at St. Athanasius's Catholic Youth Organization (CYO) team. Ferrara had played on the street in front of his apartment building and on the rock-strewn field at his school. Now Al and his CYO coach approached Ebbets Field.

Built in 1913, Ebbets Field had become the spiritual heart of Brooklyn. It was intimate, seating just over thirty-one thousand, a bandbox of a ballpark. It wasn't a jewel box, a sort of park that would have been out of keeping with its fans, but rather a cigar box. Dodger owner Charlie Ebbets hired architect Clarence Randall Van Buskirk to design a park with the sort of soaring feeling associated with movie palaces of the time. Fans entered into an eighty-foot rotunda made of Italian marble and with twelve ticket windows. There was an enormous domed ceiling featuring a chandelier made of twelve baseball bat arms holding twelve lamps designed to look like baseballs. The Italian marble tile floor featured the illustration of a baseball with "Ebbets Field" encircling it. If the rotunda was elegant, the fans were pure Brooklyn. Early on, Apple Annie held court along with Arie the truck driver, who was the real-life inspiration for the classic Brooklyn Bum. He hurled insults at his own team; it was the nature of Brooklyn to bust one's best friend's balls. By the 1930's Hilda Chester was sitting in the bleachers, clanging her cowbell, bellowing at opponents in her Brooklyn accent: "Home was never like dis, mac." She was joined by the Dodger Sym-Phony, a group of amateur musicians who would walk through the stands playing ragtime music. Standing on top of the dugout when the umpires came on the field, the musicians would play "Three Blind Mice." After an opposing player struck out, they would play "The Worms Crawl in, the Worms Crawl Out," timing the final cymbal crash for the moment when the strike victim's butt touched the bench. Some opposing players would fake sitting down and then rise up, extending the game of cat and mouse.

The second deck extended around the stadium, emphasizing the intimate nature of the park, and a scoreboard was added in the 1930s; the layout created hundreds of different angles for a ball to carom. The entire effect became that of a tiny Brooklyn street, where everyone could hear everyone else's arguments. The fans could talk with the outfielders during a pitching change; they would toss their favorite players vials of holy water; every voice in the park could be heard, and it was impossible to escape from the guy in the seat next to you. It was, in short, a community much like Brooklyn.

Of that day in 1947 Ferrara remembers, "We walked up the ramp and there was the opening to the ballpark, and all of a sudden there was this brilliant green grass. My whole life I had played on pavement and rocks, and there was a field of grass." Jackie Robinson had just joined the team. "My first baseball experience—Ebbets Field and Jackie Robinson was playing, and the fans were going nuts with the Sym-Phony and the cheering, and I started thinking, 'This is what I want to do.'"

The Bull's devotion to baseball accelerated. When he was twelve, he and his CYO teammates traveled to Erasmus Field for the league championship game. They were playing Our Lady of Hope, a team that had already beaten them with their ace, a big kid named Jaymar. Al remembers: "He was imposing. Threw harder than anyone else. How am I going to hit this guy? First time up, I struck out. I said to myself, 'What you're doing now, you aren't going to touch him.' So first pitch, I'm just going to swing when he lets the ball go. It worked. There were goal posts out in centerfield. This ball I hit went right through the goal posts. It was the longest homer ever hit there. We beat them, 2–0. That showed me what I had to do to be successful. I wasn't a natural. Somewhere along the line I had to outthink this guy. I had to make an adjustment."

Ferrara often remarks on this distinction between the naturals of the game and the mere mortals: "Willie Mays, Hank Aaron, Joe DiMaggio—these guys were naturals. See the ball, hit the ball. They couldn't tell you exactly how they did it. Me, I had to make adjustments. Every step up toward the Major Leagues, I made an adjustment."

Ferrara was on a mission to play baseball. But first he had to negotiate with his grandmother, whose desire was for him to become a classical pianist. For Italian women of her generation, motivating their children to play classical music was a divine mission. She had insisted that her daughters take lessons, and now the same man who had taught Al's aunts to play the piano—Guido Morvillo—took on the task of teaching the Bull. Morvillo walked down the middle of the street to the grandmother's apartment, a somber man in a black suit, his hands behind his back, the sort of teacher who would whack Al's hands with a stick when he made mistakes. Al's own musical tastes differed from his grandmother's and Mr. Morvillo's: "I'm living in Brooklyn. My grandma wants Van Cliburn, and I want Little Richard." One day Al secretly purchased the sheet music to "Ebb Tide." When Guido discovered it in the piano bench: whack! He was strictly classical. Eventually Al cut a deal with his grandmother: if he played piano for an hour, she would give him a quarter to use at the Coney Island batting cages. He got twenty-five swings for his quarter, but he was such a good hitter that bystanders would put in additional quarters just to watch him crush the ball.

Guido's best students played an annual concert at Carnegie Hall. Finally Al got his grandmother to agree that if he were to become Mr. Morvillo's number one student, who always played in the last slot at Carnegie Hall, his piano career would be over. He could devote himself to baseball. She agreed, and in typically compulsive and competitive Bull fashion, Ferrara practiced diligently. When he was sixteen, he was named the number one student; he closed the concert at Carnegie Hall. He stood up, took a bow in the hallowed venue—and never played piano again.

Al attended Lafayette High School, which saw an extraordinary run of talent pass through it during the 1950s. In addition to claiming alums such as Larry King, Rhea Perlman, Peter Max, Paul Sorvino, and Vic Damone, the school also graduated future Major League baseball players Bob Aspromonte, Ken Aspromonte, and, most famous of all, Sandy Koufax. Lafayette played against Brooklyn high schools that featured Joe Pepitone, Joe Torre, and Tommy Davis. Ferrara had a miserable senior year, batting .083, but somehow remained convinced that his destiny as a baseball player lay ahead. After graduation a friend of his wrangled a tryout for him with the Dodger organization at Ebbets Field. Al went along to shag fly balls for the other guys, but at the end of the tryout, he was called into the batter's box to take five swings. In the first three swings he hit the ball out of the park. The Dodgers called the next day and asked him to come back for a practice game; they wanted to see him play. He went 0–4 and thought that was the end of his tryout. But instead he got a call inviting him to join the Dodger Rookies. The Rookies were a sort of unofficial farm club of the Dodgers at the lowest level. The players were not officially signed to a Dodger contract, but they toured the eastern seaboard playing other amateur teams.

To the credit of Al Senior, he allowed his son to go play with the Rookies. Al Senior was so cheap that when Delia finally convinced him to move into a larger apartment, he found a larger, cheaper apartment. It was cheap because it was so close to the elevated train that the entire apartment shook every time a train rolled by. But while other Brooklyn kids worked during the summer of 1957, Al Senior allowed his son to pursue his passion of baseball. The Bull did well enough that summer that he was offered a scholarship to Long Island University (LIU). The athletic director there doubled as a Dodger scout, and a year later the Dodgers made an official offer to Ferrara. Al Senior insisted that the signing bonus be equal to the $9,000 scholarship Al Junior was giving up at LIU. Thus the Bull began his professional baseball career. His father supported his son in every way except for acknowledging his ability. Ferrara distinctly remembers years later getting a phone call from his father the day he hit two home runs in a Major League game. Ferrara assumed his father's unusual long-distance call was about his two homers, but his father was excited for a different reason: he had kept careful track and knew that the Bull had stayed in the big leagues the requisite number of days to qualify for a Major League pension.

During Al's junior year in high school his mother Delia suffered a stroke. She recovered from it—she was a determined woman—but had speech problems. Delia was the steady influence in the Ferrara household, Al recalls: "My mother cooked for the pastors at the rectory. Our apartment had a TV, and all the kids would gather and watch. If any kid on the block had a problem, she'd go and talk to the school. She was the peacemaker for the family and the neighborhood. My father would laugh at it—he thought there was no chance of keeping the peace. But she was the glue." After high school, when Ferrara started playing for the Dodger Rookies, he loved to bring the trophies they'd hand out to the most valuable player of a game. He'd put a trophy on the table so that she would see it in the morning: "She was so proud."

After high school Ferrara started at LIU, playing basketball and looking forward to playing baseball for in the spring of 1958.

He was seventeen. One morning when he returned from school and walked down the street toward the family apartment, he saw an ambulance; the crew was taking his mother out of the apartment. Al Senior and Al Junior thought she would recover. But at 3:30 that morning his father got a call from the hospital: Delia was dead. The Bull went downstairs and discovered his father weeping. He didn't say anything but walked to the 33 rpm record player and played "Blue Velvet" by Fats Domino. He played that song every day for months and months. A few years later his childhood friend Bobby Satriano said to him, "Kiki, Kiki, you were such a nice kid. And then when your mother died, you went crazy." At the age of seventeen Al was without the woman who had provided the boundaries for his life. He was on his own, and it began a several-decade run of wild times.

Al played two seasons with the Brooklyn Rookies and then officially signed with the Dodgers and began his Minor League career. Ferrara remembers how Minor League players learned their fate at the end of spring training in 1959: "There was one day that everyone waited for: the cut day. You'd come down into the lobby at Vero Beach. They'd put up a white sheet of paper with the Minor League rosters listed. If your name wasn't on there, you were moving on. Talk about cruelty." For the Bull in 1959 there was good news on that sheet of paper: he was going to Orlando to play in the Florida State League.

Ferrara's first Minor League team, Orlando's Class D club, paid $300 a month and a dollar a day in meal money. The team traveled on an un-air-conditioned bus to play games in Palaka, Florida: "It had snakes. There were no fences. They told you that if a guy hits a drive to left center and the ball rolled over the embankment, don't go back there. There are snakes. It was like I was back at St. Athanasius in Brooklyn—no fence. I was used to that. I wasn't used to the snakes."

At the end of the season Al had hit .270, with 8 homers. No one considered him a top prospect—except Al. He was somehow still convinced he would end up in the big leagues. That winter the Dodgers asked him to play winter ball in Panama, in a tough league loaded with older veterans of the Minor Leagues. Even though he was just nineteen, Ferrara gamely traveled to Panama City. The team stayed in the Hotel Roosevelt, its lobby lined with hookers. In Panama, Ferrara recalls, "Every damn week there was a revolution." He played for the Azucarados Sugar Kings and found himself overmatched. After about a month the Dodgers brought him back home to Brooklyn.

Al spent the winter in Brooklyn and reconnected with his high school sweetheart, Angela. Their romance grew. But the following spring the Bull reported for a second professional season. At the end of spring training Ferrara once again went to the lobby to see where he would be going: "I ran from upstairs when the list was out. In my mind I'm saying, 'I'm probably going back to D ball.' Here comes Fresco Thompson. He tells me, 'Get your dancing shoes on; you're going to Reno.'"

Al's year in Reno playing for the Silver Sox was a turning point. He made an adjustment to his hitting and suddenly was on fire. The team was in first place, a band of brothers who traveled to road games on a bus across the freezing Donner Pass on a harrowing two-lane highway that hugged the edge of a mountainous precipice. Reno itself was a wide-open city. Its casinos never closed, and most of the blackjack dealers in town were women who had come for quickie divorces and then stayed on. The Bull took full advantage. He was hitting the ball well, his team was winning the pennant, and he was getting comped into all the lounge shows. Reno was studded with classic lounge acts such as Freddy Bell and the Bell Hops. The classic stripper Lili St. Cyr played Reno—"the number one stripper of that generation," as Ferrara notes. "She'd get up there flipping her panties. Brooklyn guys had never been exposed to that situation." After he got his $300 paycheck each month, he'd play craps or blackjack and quickly bust, but it didn't matter. Because the team was doing so well, everything was on the house. Ferrara was eating whatever he wanted and enjoying life at the Clayton Rooming House. A young woman named Lodi Loda took a liking to the Bull and suggested they get together—in her bathtub. "I said, 'Wouldn't that be a little awkward, with water splashing all over the place?' She says, 'There will be no water in the bathtub.' 'Ah,' I thought to myself. 'I've heard about these people; they are called water conservationists.'"

It was in Reno that a madam gave him some memorable advice: "She said, 'Don't ever put yourself in a position to be jacked, and if you do put yourself in that position, take full responsibility for it.' I found that for the rest of my life I was always putting myself into those positions; I always seemed to put myself on the edge. But I was able to look in the mirror the next morning and take responsibility for all of it. I've had a couple of bad breaks along the way, but that's part of the game. Everybody has bad breaks." In August the owner of the Silver Sox approached the team's manager, asking him if he knew Ferrara was out until three or four in the morning. The manager replied, "He's hitting .350. Leave him alone."

As a teenager, Ferrara loved the movies and had crushes on stars like Rita Hayworth and Marilyn Monroe. The summer he was in Reno a crew came to town to film *The Misfits*. Out of the blue he saw John Huston and Clark Gable walking down the street. Then one day Ferrara opened his window in the Clayton Rooming House, looked to his left, and there was Marilyn Monroe, leaning out of a window, getting ready for a shot. She smiled and waved at the Bull. "I was floored," Al recalls. "But make no mistake—I'm not Joe DiMaggio, and she's not going to be messing with some C ballplayer. I didn't see her again."

After his season in Reno Ferrara returned to Brooklyn in the winter and impulsively proposed to Angela. They got married quickly, and the wedding proved to be an early example of Ferraranomics. The Bull had $9,000 to his name but purchased a $2,500 engagement ring. He paid for the wedding and had the reception at Vincent's Restaurant in Little Italy, with the wedding guests eating calamari and scungilli. There was tension around the ceremony. Al Senior had started dating the woman he would later marry. He wanted to bring her to the wedding, but the Paulucci side objected: "They said if she comes to the wedding, we ain't coming," the Bull remembers. "Now I had to make a decision between my grandmother and my father. There were warring factions in the family; it was splintered by my mother's loss; the glue was gone." He told his father to come alone. On the night of the wedding his best man, Bobby Genovese, argued with the band because it wanted to stop playing at the designated hour and he insisted they continue. He ended up in a fist fight with the drummer in the back room.

At Italian weddings in Brooklyn, friends would give the new couple envelopes of money. On the wedding night Ferrara and his bride went to a hotel for the honeymoon. The Bull made an excursion out of the hotel. He took the money from the envelopes, went to Madison Square Garden, and bet it on two basketball games—the Syracuse Nationals against the Knicks. He lost everything. So the marriage was not off to an auspicious start.

The following year Ferrara was assigned to the Atlanta Crackers (yes, that was the official name in 1961). Angela came with him, and their son was born. It was a difficult time for her—neither of them drove, and she was alone much of the time. It was a relief to return to Brooklyn. The next stops for Ferrara in the Minors took him to Spokane and Omaha. In 1963 the Bull was crushing the ball in Spokane. He was hitting over .300 and had 19 home runs. On July 30, Buzzie called Al "the Bull" Ferrara up to the big leagues. Ferrara's lifelong dream was realized. He called his father, who was not an outwardly emotional man, but he expressed his joy. Then the Bull called his grandmother, who asked, "Isn't Leo Durocher a coach on the Dodgers?" Ferrara said yes, and she replied, "When you get there, can you have him call me?"

Thanks to the Dodgertown experiences of spring training during the past four years, Ferrara knew his teammates. He was already good friends with Johnny Podres. But he had never been to Dodger Stadium. He arrived in Los Angeles, connected with Podres at the Mayfair Hotel, and got a ride to the ballpark. He walked into the clubhouse and saw his uniform with the number 20. Late in the game he was sent up to pinch-hit against Met pitcher Tracy Stallard. Because the Dodgers were playing the Mets, he knew the game was being broadcast back in New York, and all of his family and old Brooklyn buddies would be listening.

The Bull remembers walking up to the plate in a Major League stadium for the first time in his life. The size and the noise were a shock. "I was going, 'Jesus, there it is.' I hadn't played in a stadium like this. The lights, those banks of lights above the stadium; fifty thousand people—I was nervous as hell." Tracy Stallard struck him out. After the game the Bull went to the Embassy Bar, met a nice young lady, accompanied her to his room at the Mayfair Hotel—and got rolled. "Yeah," he mutters, "I had no money in my pocket when I woke up."

Al had had his taste of paradise in 1963, but he spent all of 1964 back in Spokane. In April 1965 he was in the big leagues again and determined to never go back to the Minors. But how could he show the Dodgers what he could do if he never played?

Finally, on Monday, April 26, he got a start. The Dodger outfield had been identical in each game up to this day: Tommy Davis, Willie Davis, and Ron Fairly. On that day Ferrara started in right field. He batted twice, drove in a run, and walked. He had made the most of this start—and in the next game he didn't play. The Dodgers, it should be noted, were winning; they were in first place for virtually the entire month. On Wednesday, April 28, Al pinch-hit for pitcher Claude Osteen in a losing cause against the Pirates. In the last two days of April he didn't play.

In the entire month of April the Bull had had five at bats. He had one hit—a triple off Spahn. But as the parent of every Little Leaguer knows, when a guy doesn't play, it's hard to get a rhythm. Five at bats is not a sample size large enough to predict anything; it's meaningless. But it meant something to Walter Alston—or rather he clearly felt that Willie Davis and Ron Fairly were better outfielders. (There was never any question about the All-Star quality of Tommy Davis, who led the league in batting in 1962 and 1963.) Buzzie Bavasi watched his team with satisfaction. The Dodgers were winning; the pitching was strong; the defense was strong. If Ferrara wanted more playing time, that was his business. Whatever was going on, the Bull was sitting on the bench. Like all athletes, he wanted to play. His frustration started to build.

May   4

On May 1, 1965, the Dodgers played the Giants, and their outfield formula remained set: Tommy Davis in left field, Willie
Davis in center, and Ron Fairly in right. But during that game a
nightmare unfolded: Tommy Davis, racing toward second base,
hit the dirt early and awkwardly, and, as he said later, "When I
looked down, I thought my ankle was in right field." His ankle
was broken, and he was done for the season. Davis never again
had the same blazing speed. He had been playing at a Hall of
Fame level, but that was gone. Who would replace him? Another
door seemed to open for Al Ferrara. Or did it?

On May 4 Al got a start. The Bull batted seventh, got a hit, and
drove in two runs. The next day he batted cleanup and went 1 for 3
with an RBI. But he was battling through an injury: playing hard,
as always, the Bull had run into the left-field wall chasing after
a ball and had hurt his hand. If he had remained healthy when
Tommy Davis went down, would the Bull have finally had his shot
as a regular starter? We will never know because a new name
entered the picture: Lou Johnson came on as a defensive replace-
ment late in the game. Sweet Lou—a veteran Minor Leaguer who
had started out in the Negro Leagues—had been called up when
Davis was injured. He was about to have the best two years of
his life. Ferrara remembers: "For two years Sweet Lou played
like Willie Mays. He was a breath of fresh air." During the next

eight games the Bull never left the dugout. Buzzie Bavasi had called up Lou Johnson, and once again he had picked a winner.

Emil "Buzzie" Bavasi was from the affluent suburb of Scarsdale, New York, but it is misleading to pigeonhole him as a scion of wealth. His father, Joseph "Frenchy" Bavasi, was born in Marseilles, France, the son of Italian immigrants who moved again in 1895 to America. Frenchy's father opened a tailor shop, and by 1910 the family was living at 348 Mott Street in Manhattan. Frenchy—an ironic name given that the family still spoke Italian in the home—married Veronica Susan Maggio on July 28, 1909, and their second child, Emil, was born December 12, 1914.

Frenchy worked as the foreman for a newspaper printer and made a brilliant realization: at that time each newspaper delivered its own product to the hundreds of newsstands around New York. It would be much more efficient to have one company deliver all of the newspapers. Frenchy borrowed $500 from J. P. Morgan's bank, bought a horse and cart, and began delivering a dozen different papers to each newsstand. Within a few years his business had grown to eighty trucks delivering papers across a territory that stretched from Long Island to New Jersey and Connecticut. To run a trucking business in New York during the Prohibition era meant rubbing elbows with tough customers, and Frenchy fended off threats from both made men and union organizers. A union boss showed up at the loading docks one day. Frenchy picked him up bodily, thrust him into an oil barrel of grease, pulled him out, and advised him that if he ever returned, Frenchy would put a match to that barrel. It was a bare-knuckles era, and Frenchy refused to back down.

Frenchy never invested in stocks, preferring to keep his money in the bank, and as the Depression deepened—and people continued to buy newspapers—the Bavasi family remained well off. So "Buzzie"—a childhood nickname after his sister said he was "always buzzing around"—grew up wealthy, but it was first-generation, hard-earned money. Buzzie and the Bull shared father figures who came from a particular Italian mold: tough men who made their own way in the world. One was wealthy, the other was not, but there was a common thread to these two childhoods.

Buzzie attended Fordham Prep. One day as he walked to catch the train to school, he saw a little girl walking up the hill, books under one arm and the other in the air as she practiced the Highland Fling. The girl was perhaps eleven, and Buzzie immediately announced that he was going to marry her. Ten years later he did. Her name was Evit Rice. For a couple that remained married for over fifty years, they had an inauspicious start. For their very first date Evit invited Buzzie to a New Year's Eve party at her home, and Buzzie forgot to go. Buzzie made amends by calling her and inviting her to go to the movies. He was on a party line, and one of Buzzie's friends had been on when the date was made. He caught Buzzie before he rang off and told him to cancel the date as there was a big bowling tournament that night. Buzzie said he couldn't do that, but the friend persisted, saying he should plead sick. Buzzie relented and agreed to call Evit back—at which point Evit, who had been on the line the whole time, said, "Don't bother; I just heard you."

Their first real date occurred when she was thirteen and he was fifteen. Evit invited Buzzie to a dance at her school. Buzzie understood that the etiquette for dating called for sending the young lady orchids, and he did so. Mr. Rice accepted the delivery with some consternation, thinking that only an older man would send orchids. He was determined to tell this guy to get lost. That night a long, stretch, twelve-cylinder Cadillac pulled up in front of the Rice home. It was Frenchy's car, driven by Fritz the chauffeur. Buzzie, dressed in white slacks and a blue blazer, got out. He knocked on the front door, and Mr. Rice answered. Mr. Rice began to laugh. Buzzie, at 5 feet 4 inches, was shorter than Evit and was not what Rice expected to see. He let them go out. That was Buzzie from an early age: focused and clear, a young man in white slacks, a blue blazer, and a bow tie.

In December 1932 Frenchy went to the hospital for a minor operation. While he was recovering, a visitor came to see him. Mr. Vandeventer had sold Frenchy a life insurance policy. But

Vandeventer had made a mistake: he had failed to get the insurance company's doctor to examine Bavasi. If the company found out his error, he would be fired. Frenchy pointed to his jacket, hanging on a rack. "The policy is in the pocket," he said. "Tear it up." He saved the man's job. January 1, 1933, was cold and snowy. But it was New Year's Day, and Frenchy decided he wanted to go home. He put on his robe, caught a cab, and returned to Scarsdale, twenty-five miles away. He came down with pneumonia and died two days later. Buzzie had lost his father.

The Bavasi family was Catholic on both sides, and Susan was determined that Buzzie attend a Catholic college. Buzzie was enrolled to attend Notre Dame. But when Buzzie returned from a dude ranch in the summer of 1933, his mother informed him that there had been a change in plans. His late father's friend Ford Frick had visited and advised her that Buzzie should attend his alma mater, DePauw University, in Greencastle, Indiana. Confusing DePauw, the Methodist school, with DePaul, the Catholic school in Chicago, Susan agreed, believing that she was sending her son off to a good Catholic university. Buzzie was happy because DePauw, unlike DePaul, was coed. The tuition was paid by the family lawyer, and no one ever told Susan otherwise. She remained in the dark as far as Buzzie could tell.

In Buzzie's sophomore year, his mother decided to attend a wedding in Chicago. The faithful Fritz drove her across the country, and they stopped to see Buzzie along the way. They arrived in Greencastle and sat down to visit in Buzzie's fraternity. They chatted for an hour before Susan announced she must get going to make it to Chicago and the wedding that evening. As she was leaving, she noticed girls on the campus and asked what they were doing there. Improvising quickly, Buzzie said that that night was the big prom, and they were visiting for the occasion. Susan asked Buzzie what band would be playing. Buzzie thought quickly and came up with a name: Shep Fields. His mother listened to Shep Fields and His Rippling Rhythm every Wednesday night out of Chicago. Buzzie was relieved that his mother bought the story and promised himself he would never lie to her again.

The next day Susan called and asked how the prom had gone. Buzzie said, "Just great," and then asked how the wedding had been. Susan replied that it had been lovely but that Shep Fields must have been a busy man because he played the wedding as well. She never said a word more about the scam.

Buzzie had an insouciant attitude toward his studies. His first roommate, Jack Oswald, who went on to be president of Penn State for nineteen years, came in one day, threw his books on the desk, and said, "Darn that geology professor of mine—he gave me a B+. That's the first I've ever had." Buzzie said, "Gee, I'm having the same problem with my Spanish professor. He gave me a B+, and that's the first I've ever had." Five minutes later Jack looked up puzzled and said, "Buzzie, we've been rooming together for six months now, and I didn't know you were a straight A student." Buzzie replied, "Jack, I never said that. I just said it was my first B+."

Buzzie and Ford Frick's son Fred were roommates for his final three years at DePauw. Buzzie was the catcher on the baseball team and was batting .450. Bill Terry, general manager of the Giants, offered him $1,500 to play for a Minor League club in Tennessee. Buzzie then did something indicative of his clear-eyed objectivity: he turned down the offer. He knew that he was slow and felt he didn't have Major League potential. How many young baseball players, given the chance to pursue such a dream, would have that kind of maturity?

Susan Bavasi held no grudge about her son's attending DePauw rather than DePaul. For his graduation she gave Buzzie a convertible and a year of freedom to do whatever he wanted to do. He took her up on the offer and cruised around America in his roadster. In March 1939 he opted to go to his mother's house in Clearwater, Florida, and take in the Dodgers' spring training. Ford Frick, now president of the National League, saw Buzzie at the game and asked him what he was doing there. When Buzzie explained that his mother had given him the year off and he had two months to go, Frick cut him short: "No, you don't. Be in my office tomorrow." "What office?" "In New York." Was it luck or fate that put Ford Frick—a baseball executive—in Buzzie's life?

He essentially directed Buzzie into the path he would follow the rest of his life: that of running a baseball team.

Buzzie ended his version of the Grand Tour and reported to Frick's office, where Frick took him to see Larry MacPhail, who was then president of the Brooklyn Dodgers. MacPhail was brilliant and erratic; Dodger manager Leo Durocher said, "There is a thin line between genius and insanity, and in Larry MacPhail's case it was sometimes so thin you could see him drifting back and forth." But Branch Rickey endorsed him for his first baseball jobs in Columbus, Cincinnati, and Brooklyn, and MacPhail built winning clubs. MacPhail was the kind of troubled baseball genius who could build up a club like the Dodgers to win pennants and simultaneously alienate the owners to the point where he was fired. He repeated this behavior with the New York Yankees, getting fired immediately after the club won the 1947 World Series. But in 1939 MacPhail was still in his ascendancy with the Dodgers, and he gave Buzzie a job as office boy. And thus his career in baseball began. Buzzie Bavasi worked in baseball over the next fifty years, a half century that saw radical changes in the game, and he was at the epicenter of it all.

From the beginning Bavasi had the opportunity to learn firsthand from one of baseball's most brilliant minds—Branch Rickey. Rickey was building the previously hapless Dodger team into an enduring powerhouse in the same way as he had done for the St. Louis Cardinals earlier. "From quantity comes quality," he would say. He launched a vast array of Minor League teams to provide a pipeline of players to the Dodgers. Bavasi quickly proved he was far more than just an office boy. Within a year he had applied for the job of business manager of the Dodgers' Americus, Georgia, Class D team, and he got the job. He and Evit had been going steady, and he asked her to join him in Georgia and get married. She made the trip, getting off at the train station with her visibly pregnant sister. The pastor who was planning on officiating at the ceremony, confused Evit's sister for the bride. He backed out of the wedding, so Buzzie and Evit got married in the one Catholic church within a hundred miles. Four hours after the wedding they were in the stands of the Americus Pioneers, watching the game. The manager of the team, Bernie DeViveiros, was the only Catholic they knew in Georgia, so he had served as best man.

Bavasi quickly got a taste of the cold and fickle nature of professional baseball. Larry MacPhail called a few weeks later and told Buzzie he was sending him Stew Hofferth, a catcher. Buzzie replied that they already had a catcher, and MacPhail told him that Hofferth wasn't coming to play; he was going to be the manager. Buzzie was shocked. "What do I do with Bernie?" he asked. The reply: "Fire him."

In typical Bavasi fashion, rather than simply leave DeViveiros in the cold, he read about another team looking for a manager, called the team, and accepted the job on behalf of DeViveiros. Then he told him that he had to take the new job because it paid fifty dollars a month more. Bernie DeViveiros never knew the real story. Buzzie treated his baseball family with the same affection and care as he did his real family. Baseball has become a corporate business; for Bavasi it was always a family business.

May 8, 1965, was a reminder of the one period in his life when Buzzie was separated from baseball and from his family. It marked the twentieth anniversary of v-e Day. Buzzie and Evit's eldest son, Peter, was born in 1942, and Buzzie was running the Durham Bulls for the Dodgers. As a father with an infant son, he didn't think he would be drafted. He was wrong. He ended up serving three years as a machine gunner in the Fifth Army, Eighty-Eighth Infantry Division, campaigning in Africa and Italy. He fought his way up the Italian peninsula, pushing back the Nazi occupying force mile by mile. Some of the toughest fighting of World War II had burned into Buzzie the value of fearlessness. In combat possessing nerves of steel became an issue of life and death. Nothing in his young life had prepared him for this. In his "as-told-to" autobiography, *Off the Record*, Buzzie covers his three years in the infantry in one paragraph:

> My draft status changed to 1-a. I went to Grand Central Station for a physical, entered the U.S. Army, and served three years as a

machine-gunner in Africa and Italy. Whereas in my civilian days I wouldn't walk across the street to get a newspaper, in the war I walked from Naples all the way to the Austrian border.

When I was discharged in 1946, Mr. Rickey named me the business manager of the Dodgers Class B farm club in Nashua, New Hampshire.

We know from letters that Evit saved that Buzzie's experience in the army was life-changing. He reported to Ft. McClellan in Alabama and immediately felt the pain of separation. Added to that was the stress of basic training. He wrote that he couldn't imagine more than 70 percent of the men in his company finishing this cycle: "Can you see me walking 27 miles with a 45 lb. pack, plus a rifle?" He did that. The life-and-death stakes of the service were immediately before him: "Just before we arrived a boy was crawling on his stomach, bombs bursting all about him, machine gun bullets hitting the dirt in front of him, all of a sudden he came face to face with a snake—he had to choose between the snake and bullets. It was the last choice he ever made and it was a poor one—correct, he chose the bullets."

Buzzie quickly changed his outlook on life: "There is only one thing I want out of life now—and that is to spend the rest of it close to you and Peter. If and when this thing is over we three are going to have a lot of fun. We'll do it on little or nothing, but we'll do it. Life is too short to be wasting it on things we don't want to do."

The Eighty-Eighth Division trained statewide during 1943. But by Christmas of that year, Buzzie knew he would be headed out for actual combat soon. On Christmas day, he wrote an extraordinary letter to one-year-old Peter. His letter, written as if the infant could understand it, summarizes the essential message a father can leave his son:

DECEMBER 25, 1943

Dear Son,

Received your thoughtful Christmas gift today and I must say that it arrives at a most opportune time. I was beginning to feel sorry for myself, but one look at your happy face made me realize just why I was here at Fort McClellan. I've seen so little of you, Son, that it is hard to believe that you actually belong to me. Someday, after this horrible thing is over, we'll get to know each other real well. You know—your mother and I had Dads once, too. They were swell guys, both of them. I'll try hard to live up to their respective reputations. It will be hard at first, but bear with me and a little cooperation at times will help. You see being a father is comparatively new to me, but I'll learn as time goes by.

I understand, from your mother that you've been a real man and have been no trouble whatsoever. Keep up the good work, Son. Makes it easy on Mom and relieve[s] me of all unnecessary worry.

I learned yesterday that it is a privilege to be fighting for this great nation of ours. It is all of that, Peter—and as you grow older you will realize it all the more. I only hope and pray that you will never have to take part in anything as terrible as this— the worst part being away from your loved ones.

Peter, the first thing I want you to realize is that you must tolerate everyone and bear with the mistakes of others. One or two men make mistakes and millions of men must give up their lives to make amends—if you and boys your age learn the right way of living at an early stage there will be no wars to bring grief to the world—

Your education shall be second to none, Son, but after that it is up to you.

Goodnight—and remember that I expect big things of you.

Love
Dad

Peter Bavasi looks at this letter today, over seventy years later, and is taken with his father's unyielding belief in tolerance and forgiveness. Buzzie would be instrumental in signing and nurturing the careers of Don Newcombe and Roy Campanella, who followed Jackie Robinson's path to the Majors, but there was no way he could have known that on Christmas Day 1943. Peter looks at the letter today and says, "Baseball is a game of forgiveness and redemption. You're having a bad night. You strike out three times with runners on base. But then you hit the game-winning home run. You are forgiven; you are redeemed. And in a large sense it is a game of tolerance. Buzzie believed in that with all his heart."

When the brutal struggle was finally over, Buzzie allowed himself one letter that honestly depicted the horrors he saw:

Honey, I'm tired, worn out and unhappy. Guess the army has finally made many changes in me. I'm actually afraid of myself now. Wish you were here so I could sit and talk to you. I need you badly now—as never before. . . . Maybe I shouldn't tell you these things, but the average civilian thinks a doughboy is a robot with no feelings. Last winter, on October 1st to be exact, 21 of us went up on Mt. Battaglia and dug in for six days, beating off five fierce enemy counterattacks. On October 6th we were relieved by the British and only five of us came down from the Mountain. Not a good percentage is it, honey. The night after the initial attack on Monterumici we were able to count only 76 heads out of 186. Many a time I've seen men pray that shells would start coming in so that they could hit the dirt and get a minute's rest. During the push through the Gothic Line, which took 50 of the most uncomfortable days imaginable, I saw men blown limb from limb 30 feet into the air. No I'm not exaggerating, it's the truth. I'd like to see some of those politicians sleeping in a fox hole knee deep in water. No, baby, it hasn't been fun.

This is all for now as it is getting near chow time and although I'm not hungry we might have some ice cream. Italian variety, which we buy out of the company fund. Not good—but cold.

I love you *very very very very much.*

Buzzie

In 1946 Buzzie Bavasi was honorably discharged from the army. Peter Bavasi says he never heard his father speak of his experience in World War II.

Now, twenty years later, Buzzie was the general of a baseball team, shaping its personnel and overall strategy. Compared to what he saw in World War II, it was indeed a child's game, but for the players—young men trying to make a living and become the heroes they imagined themselves to be—it was deeply serious. On May 8, 1965, the Dodgers were playing the Giants in Candlestick Park, and twenty-three-year-old Derrell Griffith was the starting left fielder. The Bull was sitting out another game. The Dodgers won.

The month of May rolled on, Sweet Lou Johnson got hot, and Ferrara continued to play sporadically. Then came one of those days that baseball players remember their entire lives, the moment when every childhood dream is realized.

The Bull had been playing with an injury. In May, racing to get to a ball that had rolled up against the left-field fence, he put his hand up to stop his momentum. It strained the hand, and Doc Mattei wrapped it up in a bandage. On Saturday, May 15, the Dodgers were at home facing the Cubs, and Dick Ellsworth was pitching for the Cubs. Ferrara had collected his first Major League hit off Ellsworth back in 1963, but on this day Ellsworth was superb. He was pitching a no-hitter, nursing a 1–0 lead, into the bottom of the eighth inning. Then he walked a man, and the next batter laid down a sacrifice bunt. That bunt was misplayed for an error, so the Dodgers had men on first and third. Walter Alston looked down the bench and asked the Bull, "Are you okay to hit?" Ferrara instantly ripped the bandage off his hand and got a bat.

Al went to the plate. It was a sold-out crowd, a day game, a 1–0 game, and a no-hitter in the making. He knew Ellsworth was a sinker ball pitcher, but Ferrara was a low ball hitter. Ellsworth wound and delivered his first pitch—"a hell of a sinker." The Bull swung, and his hand hurt a bit as he gimped a little foul ball. Ferrara thought to himself, "You gotta get this guy." The next pitch was a sinker up just a little bit higher, and Ferrara hit a shot that landed in the left-field stands for a three-run home run. It was the only hit of the game. "Rounding those bases I was sort of numb," the Bull recalls. "This was the moment, the type of situation where people were going crazy, everybody rooting and saying, 'I hope this guy can hit a fly ball and get the guy in from third to at least tie the game.' But instead—a three-run homer."

Alston made a double switch, and the Bull went out to play left field in the top of the ninth. The whole pavilion stood up. Al muses: "I always said the guys in left field were my boys, and my homeboys from East LA sitting out there, and it was just a great feeling." Ron "Perry" Perranoski came on in relief and secured the win. The headline in the paper the next day was "The Day of the Bull." It was the highlight of Al Ferrara's baseball career.

That night Ferrara invited Perranoski to join him in Chinatown at the Dynasty Bar to celebrate. The Dynasty was a private club, steeped in mystery. Situated in the middle of old Chinatown, customers entered from the street, went down a dim corridor, and then went up a shaft elevator. The elevator was tiny, dark, and seemed to lead nowhere. Then the doors opened on an exotic bar with the feeling of a speakeasy. The Bull and Perry had a couple of cocktails, and then Perranoski drove Ferrara to his home in the San Fernando Valley. Perranoski took the wheel because (as noted) as a native New Yorker, the Bull had yet to learn how to drive a car. He hustled rides to the ballpark from teammates, from dates of the previous night, from friends, and occasionally from complete strangers he met in a hotel lobby when the Dodgers were playing away games. As was always the case, Ferrara lived on the edge and seemed to relish life as an improvisation. The Dynasty Bar, the Bull's not knowing how to drive a car: these elements would return all too soon to haunt the 1965 season.

But on that glorious May 15 there was only the thrill of the game-winning homer, the dim warmth of the Dynasty, and then the conviviality of an impromptu party at Perranoski's home. Perranoski had come to the Dodgers through one of Buzzie's trades, the process of which he detailed in a four-part *Sports Illustrated* series he did in 1967 with sportswriter Jack Olsen. Just before the 1960 season Buzzie got a call from Bing Devine, the Cardinals GM,

who was looking to acquire Don Zimmer. Zim was one of Buzzie's favorites (and a great friend of the Bull), but Buzzie felt that
he was "approaching that period where he still looked valuable,
but he was beginning to lose the touch and it [was] the perfect
time, in other words, to trade him." Devine offered Buzzie $25,000
for Zimmer. Buzzie said he'd call him back and promptly got on
the phone with the Chicago Cubs GM John Holland and manager
Charlie Grimm. Buzzie told them Zimmer was available, and Holland was interested. He asked what ballplayers Buzzie wanted in
a trade, and Buzzie replied, "I don't know. Who you got?" Holland offered outfielder Lee Handley and Johnny Goryl, the second
baseman. Then he mentioned a couple of players Buzzie wasn't
interested in before saying, "We've got a pretty good-looking left-
hander coming out of the army." "Named what?" "Perranoski. P-e-
r-r-a-n-o-s-k-i." Buzzie said he'd never heard of him, and Charlie
Grimm piped up, "Well, we gave him $30,000 to sign. That's who
he is." Buzzie thought if they had given him that much, he couldn't
be all bad, so he took him. He cited this case as an example of the
large role luck plays in making deals. But luck starts with initiative, and Buzzie was always entrepreneurial.

In 1965 Perranoski was the established closer for the team.
Like virtually everyone on the Dodgers, he relished Ferrara's
company: "Al was a great teammate. He came every day ready
to play. He kept everyone loose in the clubhouse and was always
prepared to play." Perry, as he was called, threw fabulous parties, with memorable hors d'oeuvres. He was one of those players who not only had a great baseball life, but also knew people
all over town. He did Dodge commercials, and there were friends
from the car business; there were baseball buddies both on and
off the field, and there were show business pals. The party at his
house went on late into the night, and in the morning Perry's
two young sons ran up to their father's bedroom to tell him that
"Uncle Bull is here." Ferrara had passed out in the guest bedroom, happy and a hero.

Perry and the Bull arrived at Dodger Stadium early the next
day for a Sunday doubleheader. Ferrara remembers that Buzzie

came down to the clubhouse with his good friend Dr. Robert Kerlan, the orthopedic surgeon. He busted the Bull's chops, asking him how things were going. They were going great; life was good. "It was just a wonderful two days, those two days," the Bull summed up.

Then the Dodgers played their doubleheader. Ferrara did not get an appearance in either game. Asked how he felt about that fifty years later, Ferrara replied, "I'm only giving you the facts. Look, people got reasons to do everything. I would hope that the reason [I didn't play] was because we had five better outfielders and not that Alston didn't want to play somebody who had drunk the night before."

The Bull didn't play the following game either. Finally, on May 19, he pinch-hit—unsuccessfully. That same day Lou Johnson went 4 for 6. About the rest of the month Ferrara remembered, "I ain't doing so hot, playing sporadically. Lou is playing good." He pinch-hit occasionally, got an rbi, scored a run, but didn't play much. Meanwhile, Lou Johnson ended the month of May batting .306, and the Dodgers ended the month in first place, three games ahead of the Giants.

Baseball has a unique quality of being a team game that shines a fierce spotlight on the individual: one man is the pitcher, and he is held personally responsible for winning or losing a game (the pitcher takes the win or the loss, after all). One man stands at the plate with the chance to get a hit, maybe win the game, or maybe end the game by going down swinging. In May Al Ferrara had his finest moment in the spotlight. In June he would have his worst, but it came off the field, not on.

June

5

Two days after the Bull's triumphant home run, Clark Clifford, chairman of the president's Intelligence Advisory Board, wrote to Lyndon Johnson with a warning about the war in Vietnam: "This could be a quagmire." Two weeks earlier the Rolling Stones had played a concert in Clearwater, Florida, in which hundreds of their fans had mixed it up with police officers, and the Stones had to leave the stage after playing just four songs. The Ike Age society, which had dominated America during the 1950s with its strictures of corporate propriety, was undergoing a seismic shift.

Baseball, which has always offered a mirror of sorts to American society, was not immune to this cultural earthquake. The Los Angeles Dodgers in particular inhabited a special place in America's consciousness. The Dodgers, after all, were the one sports team that had played an active role in the battle for civil rights. They were one of the teams that had led the march west, pointing to California as the new promised land of the American dream. The Dodgers of the 1960s may have been the last innocents, as Michael Leahy's excellent book titles them, but they were aware of the transition churning around them.

"We were a different generation," says Ferrara. In 1966 attorney Marvin Miller first visited Major League training camps to empower the players' union, but the feelings he tapped were already in motion in 1965. Ferrara felt Miller symbolized the 1960s as a time of revolution. Miller's first meeting with the Dodgers is imprinted in the Bull's memory: "Here's this little guy, guy half my size, got a mustache, got a bad arm. Arm dangled off to one side. First thing he said, 'You are the dumbest sons of bitches I've ever seen. Topps Bubble Gum gives you a hundred bucks when you make the Major Leagues. They are a million dollar organization. The kids that buy Topps aren't buying the bubble gum that goes with the card. They are buying your picture.'" Such a rhetorical approach was not that far from Walter Alston's. In both cases the goal was to motivate the ball players, and in both cases it seems to have worked. Within five years the players had a new contract that put in place arbitration procedures for resolving disputes between a player and an owner. The first step toward freedom from contractual servitude had been taken.

How did this revolution play with Buzzie Bavasi? As he looked for players with nerves of steel, did those nerves include the temerity to stand up to ownership? He would live through the evolution of the free agency era, and in his autobiography, *Off the Record*, he expressed his regrets about how the game changed as a result: "I see businessmen in knickers hoping to get rich quick from a game that was meant to be played for fun. I see agents taking millions of dollars out of the game and never putting a dime back into it." This reflects the old sportsman-owner tradition (or, more frequently, myth) that owners put the money they earned from the game back into their teams and parks, improving the experience for the fans. Fair enough; no agents have ever allocated a commission into a fund for improved seating for the fans (although that's not their job). Bavasi wrote, "I was in baseball for 45 years and I never had an ulcer, because I enjoyed what I was doing."

June 1965 marked an internal change in baseball that made a significant and lasting change in the game: Major League baseball held its first amateur free-agent draft. Up until then a young player out of high school or playing in college could sign with whomever he wished. It was free enterprise at work, but the invisible hand of the marketplace had an odd way of favoring the wealthiest clubs—in particular the New York Yankees. They had the money to outbid other clubs, and a vicious cycle was born over the decades: the Yankees grabbed the best young talent, won world championships, had an enormous fan base in the largest American market, and made a ton of money with which they could buy the next generation of young talent. This theoretic mastery of free enterprise was layered over the bizarre pre-capitalism/feudalism of baseball before the free-agent era. Players were signed to contracts from which there was no escape; the Major League team that owned them (and "owned" is the appropriate word here) could trade them, demote them, and dictate their salaries. The whole system was predicated on the so-called reserve clause, which had evolved in the late nineteenth century to prohibit players from moving from team to team. For eighty years the reserve clause had essentially bound players to the team they had signed with for perpetuity. Within five years Curt Flood would take a case to the Supreme Court to overturn the reserve clause. While he didn't win the case, it set the stage for the 1972 strike, in which the players achieved binding arbitration for contract disputes. And from there free agency was just three years away. But in 1965 the reserve clause was still in full force, and wealthy teams still dominated the marketplace. With all of that in place it was a GM's job to figure out how to compete with the dominance of the Yankees and somehow triumph over the six-hundred-pound gorilla who sat atop the baseball market.

Buzzie Bavasi had inherited an enormous farm system from the Branch Rickey era. During the 1940s and '50s the Dodgers had over twenty farm teams producing a steady stream of talent. From a peak of twenty-six Minor League teams in 1948, by 1965 the Dodgers had just seven Minor League affiliates, but the culture of a quality farm system was inbred in the organization. Buzzie Bavasi continued the tradition of staffing the Minor League teams with stern taskmasters who bred into their players his prized quality of fearlessness. Minor League skipper Clay Bryant was the epitome of the Dodger insistence on excellence. He was famous for expressing his disapproval of poor play during a game by sitting on the valuables box after the game ended; nobody could get their wallets. The message was clear: second-best efforts were not acceptable. The Dodger organization was full of coaches like Bryant who had worked for the organization for twenty years. The Dodgers of the 1960s were full of players who had learned the craft coming up through the Minors—like the Bull.

Buzzie Bavasi was also a master of the second art in building a team, a skill that is hidden from the view of the public: managing baseball scouts. The mid-century baseball scout, traveling across the country in a beat-up car and finding hidden talent in obscure farm towns, has become an American icon, celebrated in novels and movies. But what few appreciate is that a baseball GM has to be able to play three-dimensional chess in handling and evaluating the scouts themselves. Like players, each scout has a particular skill set. And it's the GM's job to know the personality of each scout and the unique perspective he brings to the job. The 1960s Dodgers had a cadre of veteran scouts: John Terry, Leon Hamilton, Burg Wells, Guy Wellman, and Ed Liberatore (among many others). Each could be deployed strategically, and Buzzie was a master of such deployment as well. Leon Hamilton, for instance, was an acknowledged virtuoso of the genre known as the "parlor scout." He had a genius for negotiating with a prospective player's parents in the front parlor.

Peter Bavasi, who worked alongside his father in the 1960s, remembers Hamilton's techniques well: "Leon would go and dig and dig—he'd romance the mother, dance with her, whatever it took. Or he'd be dramatic: 'If you don't sign today, then I'm going to take this money. I can only offer you this amount until Friday, and then I have to go into my own pocket, and my kids won't have new shoes.'"

One of Hamilton's favorite tricks was to feign that he was about to leave town and give the prospect and his parents a firm deadline that didn't actually exist. He would go to a hardware store, buy a hundred-pound sack of concrete, and put it in the trunk of his car so that it appeared weighted down with luggage. He would take a few shirts out of his suitcase and hang them in the back seat. Then he'd drive to the prospect's house and solemnly announce that he was headed out of town. He'd gesture to the car, weighted with the cement and dressed with shirts. "I'm headed up country. I've got other prospects to sign. I've got my luggage in the trunk. I'm leaving right now. This is your last chance to sign the contract before I head off." The young prospect would typically sign on the dotted line, and Hamilton would return the concrete to the hardware store, get his money back, hang his shirts back up in his hotel room, and notch another signing.

Buzzie was the architect of all of such strategies. He would pull together disparate pieces of information from scouts across the country and internationally. He might be pondering, "What do I need to put us over the top? I need a reliever." He would then analyze the various scouting reports. Buzzie had complete trust in his group of scouts, relying on them to provide insights not just about prospects, but also about the Dodger team itself. He would frequently bring a scout in from the road to look at the Dodgers and identify needs on the club. The scout would see the team, understand what it was missing, and then return to his territory and find players that could fill the need. Peter Bavasi recalls many times when a scout would then call up Buzzie from Spokane or Reno to say, "There are a couple of guys on this club that could help you. They're good. One got arrested for a bar fight, but irrespective of that, this guy is hot right now. Bring him up."

Dodger scouts loved their jobs because they knew their reports were appreciated; their opinion was valued. As Peter Bavasi says, "That was almost better than money for scouts." There wasn't a debate in the organization between the scouting bureau and a GM who doubted what his scouts saw. In addition, Buzzie knew not to ask his field manager about players, either his own or opposing players. Bavasi felt that if a player did well against the manager's club, the manager would report, "That guy is terrific." If the man played badly against the club, then the response became, "That guy can't play; he stinks." Bavasi realized that his own field manager became myopic during the course of a season. He was very good at managing the club, but his abilities of observation became clouded by personal experience.

Bavasi learned much of this from Branch Rickey. Rickey was a visionary, a teacher, and a notorious cheapskate. People held Rickey in awe, calling him the Mahatma. Peter Bavasi remembers Rickey's bushy eyebrows and intense look—and the fact that he often had soup stains on his clothing. In typical Rickey fashion, he would go to lunch with Fresco Thompson and then explain, "I didn't pick up the check from the table, Fresco." Thompson would reply, "That's all right; the cashier can figure out what you ate; just show him your tie."

Cultural revolutions are entwined with personal ones, and in 1965 Al Ferrara was in the midst of personal turmoil. His youthful marriage to Angela had been fraying over the years he had spent in the Minor Leagues. Everything conspires against marriage for a young baseball player: the endless travel, the uncertainty of the profession, the temptations of the road. Al and Angela had a son, and the constant moving from city to city was challenging. Finally, when Ferrara landed in Los Angeles for good and established himself at the Mayfair Hotel, the marriage dissolved. The Bull began dating strippers he met at the El Rancho Strip Club, which in that era featured entertainers in the classic Gypsy Rose Lee tradition, such as Tornado Tanja Dorn and Leta Paul (voted Miss Striptease of Los Angeles). Among the artists there was the novelty stripper Baby Jane. The Bull recalls Baby Jane as standing just under four and a half feet and weighing north of 250 pounds: "She would go out there and do the whole strip act just like the other girls—you know how they did it in those days; they came up with furs on and delicately took their gloves off. Not like today." Another Dodger player was seeing one of the other strippers at the time, and she jealously thought her Dodger might stray on her while she was doing her show. She appointed Baby Jane to guard the player, but it proved to be a case of the wolf guarding the hen house. (Later the El Rancho was purchased by Mickey Hargitay, the actor and Mr. Universe who married Jayne Mansfield.)

The El Rancho formed part of what the Bull affectionately called his "Casbah." The Mayfair Hotel was one leg of the stool, the El Rancho another, and a third leg was Monty's Bar, which featured go-go dancers in the front room and provided a haven for card games in the back. The Mayfair was the center of action: a guy could get anything he wanted at the Mayfair. The players hung out there after games; fans knew it and would congregate there too. When there was a party, which happened during virtually every home stand, the Bull would pose the question: "Which suite do we rent—the Governor's or the President's?"

As if the Dodgers had a tail stream of Times Square that followed them to Los Angeles, Runyonesque characters popped up at the Mayfair. Three-Nickel Red (he always left the same tip—three nickels) was a friend until Ferrara gave him twenty dollars to bet on a horse that came in a winner at 17–1. Three-Nickel Red and the Bull's money were never seen or heard from again. The parking valet Andre doubled as the bar singer. One night Ferrara and Andre got into an alcohol-fueled tussle. Words were exchanged, blows were struck, and Ferrara cut his hand on a broken glass. He got stitched up in the emergency room; at the ballpark the next day he put a batting glove over the bandage to hide it. In batting practice the wound began to trickle blood, but the Bull wasn't concerned because he didn't think he was going to play. But as luck would have it, Ferrara was in the lineup that night. Almost immediately an opposing batter hit a low line drive to left-center. Ferrara raced in, dove, and collided with the center fielder. The collision brought the trainer out, as well as Don Drysdale. Blood was coming from the Bull's hand, and the trainer took off the batting glove, revealing the cut with the suture. Drysdale said, "Who stitched him up so soon?" Of course the truth came out, and Ferrara's reputation for playing hard on and off the field was burnished. (It was no surprise that Drysdale was the one who ran out, concerned. Ferrara says that for a dictionary definition of "Major Leaguer," one could write "Don Drysdale." The consummate professional, Drysdale was an intense competitor on the mound and a loving teammate in the clubhouse.)

On the fringes of the Casbah were Vincent Paul's Steak House and Langer's Deli, as well as Virginia's, which featured Latin music, Latin women, and a dance floor. The Bull loved his Casbah, which, if one expanded the map a bit, included the Dynasty Bar. He frequently took his friend JoAnne Diero there. She was an early free spirit, a woman who had a career in Mexico as a professional bullfighter and would show up with her hair dyed purple one day and green the next. She was fearless; she carried a scar from a bullfight in which she had been gored. Her parents were business people who owned three buildings on historic Olvera Street. She was the black sheep of her family, notable in part for her remarkable imitation of a wolf howl. Guys on the team called her "Wolfie" and would ask her to cut loose after a game. She would oblige, tilt back her head, and bay at the moon outside Dodger Stadium. She and Ferrara had a tempestuous relationship; she told him later that following their fights she stuck pins in a voodoo doll that represented him. Maybe this potent magic accounted for the tumultuous year of ups and downs.

On the field Koufax and Drysdale were going about their business in June 1965, pitching complete-game wins and keeping the Dodgers in first place. Ferrara started seven games between June 4 and 18. He was still sputtering mid-month in terms of his hitting, but on June 16 in a game against the Giants he got a hit, and on Friday, June 18, he went 2 for 4 and scored a run. Maybe he was finally building momentum.

Sunday, June 20, began well for the Bull. The Dodgers were playing a doubleheader at home against the Mets, and he was in the starting lineup. Being a part-time player, a guy who shows up every day not knowing whether he's going to play or not, carries a special pressure. An established everyday player knows that if he has a bad day, there will be a chance at redemption the next. If a part-timer plays poorly one day, he doesn't know when he'll get the next chance to prove that one game was an anomaly. The part-time player has to live with insecurity and has to live on the edge, as Ferrara did his entire life. In 1965 the Bull didn't have the luxury of acceptance; he fought for every at bat and every moment on the field. And while he enjoyed his life off the field, when there was a day game, he was always meticulous about getting rest the night before. A starting spot was an affirmation, and he was always determined to put out 110 percent and make the best of it.

In the first game on that Sunday the opposing pitcher for the Mets was Warren Spahn. The future Hall of Famer was forty-four years old. He was already the winningest left-handed pitcher of all time, and he was nearing the end of his career. Despite his age and his pitching for a woeful team, Spahn remained the brilliant tactician on the mound who employed his mantra effectively: "Hitting is timing. Pitching is upsetting timing." Sandy Koufax was pitching for the Dodgers, and it was a classic nerves-of-steel win: Koufax allowed just one hit and one run over a complete game, and the Dodgers won, 2–1. Ferrara went hitless in three at bats.

It was a disappointment, but for once there was an opportunity for instant redemption: the Bull was starting in game two. In today's baseball world there are virtually no true doubleheaders. Teams occasionally play two games in one day as a day-night doubleheader, but those are almost always situations in which a previously scheduled game that had been rained out is being made up. The ballpark is cleared, and the team sells another stadium full of tickets. In 1965 doubleheaders were still common. Two games for the price of one; the second game would commence shortly after the first one had ended. Baseball, after all, is not like football or basketball. Nine innings don't deplete position players completely. The mental stress of playing eighteen innings in one day takes perhaps a greater toll than the physical exhaustion. On June 20 Ferrara was getting to play eighteen innings in one day.

In game two the Dodgers faced off against veteran Frank Lary. When Lary tired, reliever Larry Miller came in. The Mets came from behind to win, 3–2. Ferrara got one hit in the losing effort. And he made an error. He had worked hard on his fielding. When he played in Spokane, manager Preston Gomez had Ferrara come to the ballpark at 3:30 every day, and Gomez would spend an hour and a half hitting balls to Ferrara in right field. Gomez was a great fungo hitter—a very specific skill—and he would pummel the Bull, dropping fly balls with pinpoint accuracy, knowing just how to make Ferrara run from right to left and then back up or charge the ball. Fielding fly balls was one defensive issue; the other was Ferrara's arm. When healthy, Ferrara had a strong throwing arm. The problem was that for several seasons he played through various stages of a sore arm. On June 20, in the second game, he made an error in the outfield, and it upset him. Ferrara had played two full games, gone 1 for 7, and seen his team lose the second game. "I booted the ball—it was just a miserable day," he concluded. The Bull's baseball day was done.

After the game Al met JoAnne. They often went to Hollywood to see singer Trini Lopez at PJ's. But Ferrara wasn't in the mood to hear "If I Had a Hammer." They went to the Dynasty in Chinatown instead. The dark bar with its comforting mysterious ambience was more in line with the Bull's mood. They had some drinks. They walked out of the Dynasty, and Ferrara said, "I'm driving." JoAnne looked at him in surprise.

"You don't drive."

"I'm driving."

Years later, Ferrara admits he had no idea why he said this or why it happened. It was an impulsive choice, perhaps a way to feel in control of something after an afternoon in which he had controlled very little. At approximately 10 p.m. they got into JoAnne's car—again, it would be years before the Bull actually learned how to drive—and took off. Ferrara made a left turn and discovered he was going up the Hollywood Freeway exit ramp the wrong way. In a case of some higher power possessing both a sense of safety and a sense of humor, as he swerved onto the freeway, he nearly ran into a police car. The officers promptly pulled him over, and he was arrested. They took him to the station, and Ferrara posted a $276 bail. As sportswriter Bob Hunter wrote, "The Bull's car had been drinking."

The next day, when he arrived at the ballpark, Buzzie called him into his office and read him the riot act. Walter Alston called a team meeting after batting practice and read the entire team the riot act. And then, strangely, Ferrara was in the starting lineup once again. He remembers the game on June 21 vividly. He was facing starting pitcher Alvin Jackson; it was a 1–0 game, another classic Dodgers low-scoring nerves-of steel-contest. Late in the game the Bull hit a shot down the left-field line. It curved foul just before it reached the foul pole, a foot away from being a home run. Ferrara muses, "I always wondered if the ball would've hit that foul pole and won the game, things might have changed. I don't know. . . ." He knew that as a marginal player a stricter standard was applied to him. A superstar could get away with drinking, carousing, and bar fights (consider Mickey Mantle), and nothing would happen. But for a guy batting under .200, the ice was very thin. The next day Ferrara's arrest hit the newspapers. Buzzie again called Ferrara into his office. He was apoplectic. Buzzie's anger was legendary: he was famous for exploding; then the volcano would suddenly subside, and he would be completely calm. In this meeting he blew up, and the calm came only after the meeting. Buzzie told Ferrara he was sending him to Spokane and that he would never play for the Dodgers again. The *Los Angeles Times* quoted Buzzie: "If Ferrara were Babe Ruth or someone like that and was helping the team it might be different, but a .189 hitter can't afford to get out of line." So the Bull's analysis was correct: the scales of justice would always tilt toward Babe Ruth. And he wasn't playing like Babe Ruth.

What Ferrara did next was the actualization of his characteristic gesture—the wiping of the hands and moving on. He immediately flew up to Spokane and was ready to play the team's next game. Players didn't do this. Management assumed that an angry or disappointed player demoted to the Minors would take a few days to report. Ferrara got on a plane, showed up in Spokane, and was ready to play. Years later Buzzie told the Bull he couldn't believe that Ferrara was playing in Spokane the next day. Ferrara explains: "I was a baseball player. I was a screw-up, but I was a baseball player. The first love was always the game."

Always the optimist, Al still hoped he could return to the Majors and get a World Series ring. The Bull was heart stricken, but he never gave up. In Buzzie's mind, as of June 22 the Bull was exiled from Valhalla, probably for life. At least that is what he stated in the heat of the moment. As he looked at his team on June 22, he saw a club in first place but riddled with injuries. *The Sporting News* ran a cartoon by Karl Hubenthal showing Lady Bird Johnson informing her husband, the president, that on the phone "someone in Los Angeles wants to know where he can apply for Medicare." And in a phone booth making that call was an amalgam Dodger player with injuries to his ankle (Tommy Davis), shoulder (Wes Parker), back (John Roseboro), knee (Don Drysdale), ribs (Willie Davis), thumb (Lou Johnson), and (the crowning blow) the elbow (Sandy Koufax). These men were playing through their injuries, in true nerves-of-steel fashion, but it was taking a toll. They were in first place but ranked ninth in the National League in runs scored. Buzzie had launched the season vowing an offensive upgrade at third base. Veteran Jim "Junior" Gilliam was moved to the first base coaching box, and John Kennedy, acquired in the Frank Howard trade, started the season at third. But after ten games Kennedy looked overmatched at the plate. Dick Tracewski started for about a month and was hitting no better. After a stretch of thirty scoreless innings Bavasi called a meeting of the coaching staff. He proposed that they reactivate Jim Gilliam. Gilliam shot him a look: "You picked a fine night to bring me back." They were playing the Cardinals, and Bob Gibson was pitching. Bavasi responded: "Wait until tomorrow." Gilliam returned and immediately started hitting well. His defense was always impeccable and would prove life-saving at the end of the long year. Another pleasant surprise was the emergence of Sweet Lou Johnson as a star. It didn't offset Tommy Davis's season-ending injury, but it provided a much-needed spark.

What Buzzie could not have anticipated was that the summer of 1965 would blossom into a watershed for the civil rights movement. As the Bull picked up the pieces of his life in Spokane, the city of Los Angeles was entering the heart of a long, hot, summer.

1. Buzzie Bavasi poses with
three Brooklyn Dodger Hall of
Famers signing their contracts:
(*left to right*) Pee Wee Reese, Roy
Campanella, and Jackie Robinson.
(Bettmann/Getty Images)

2. During World War II Buzzie Bavasi was a machine-gunner in the front lines with "the Blue Devils"—the U.S. Army's Eighty-Eighth Infantry Division, which battled its way up the Italian peninsula. He was awarded a Bronze Star for meritorious service in combat at the Mount Battaglia, San Clemente, and Po Valley campaigns. While in Rome, he met up with Ethan Allen, who is holding *The Sporting News*. Allen had signed on with the Army Special Service Sports Troupe and ran a baseball clinic at the Rest Center in Rome. (Bavasi Family Archives)

3. (*opposite top*) In June 1945 Buzzie Bavasi, Ethan Allen, and Charlie Hass examine a massive statue of a catcher, erected in Rome at the American Rest Center. (Bavasi Family Archives)

4. (*opposite bottom*) On September 29, 1964, Buzzie Bavasi (*left*) announced that manager Walter Alston had been rehired for the 1965 season. Bavasi had fought for the Brooklyn Dodgers to hire Alston as their manager in 1954; Alston had never previously managed at the Major League level. The next year he would lead the Brooklyn Dodgers to their first—and only—world championship in Brooklyn. (AP Photo/Harold Filan)

5. Al Ferrara posing in Dodger Stadium. In a trademark gesture, his index finger is lifted from the bat. (Los Angeles Dodgers)

6. (*opposite top*) The 1965 Dodgers at Dodger Stadium. The famous "Three Sisters" palm trees are visible at the left. Al Ferrara is in the middle row, the fourth player from the left. (Los Angeles Dodgers)

7. (*opposite bottom*) The Dodgers were stocked with outstanding outfielders in 1965: (*left to right*) the speedster Willie Davis, veteran Ron Fairly, "Sweet" Lou Johnson (who had the best season of his life that year), Al Ferrara, and two-time National League batting champion Tommy Davis. (Los Angeles Dodgers)

LOS ANGELES DODGERS

Top Row: left to right: Howie Reed, Maury Wills, John Kennedy, Jim Brewer, Lou Johnson, Sandy Koufax, Carroll Beringer, Batting practice pitcher; Mike Kekich, Willie Crawford.

Middle Row: Wayne Anderson, Trainer; Lee Scott, Traveling Secretary; Hector Valle, Claude Osteen, Dick Tracewski, Al Ferrara, Jeff Torborg, Ron Perranoski, John Purdin, Wes Parker, Willie Davis, Jim Lefebvre, Johnny Podres, Nobe Kawano, Equipment Mgr.; Bill Buhler, Trainer.

Bottom Row: Wally Moon, Ron Fairly, John Roseboro, Jim Gilliam, Player-Coach; Lefty Phillips, Coach; Walt Alston, Mgr.; Danny Ozark, Coach; Preston Gomez, Coach; Bob Miller, Don Drysdale.

Front: Larry Goldstein, Ballboy; Herb Aspell, Batboy. (Not shown in photo — Tommy Davis)

8. (*opposite top*) Al Ferrara is greeted by Willie Crawford (43), Maury Wills, and Dick Tracewski (44) after his game-winning home run on May 15, 1965. Ferrara's home run broke up Dick Ellsworth's no-hitter in the eighth inning. The Dodgers won the pennant that year by just two games, and this early-season win made the difference of one of those games. (Los Angeles Dodgers)

9. (*opposite bottom*) On the eve of the 1965 World Series Buzzie Bavasi sports a Minnesota Twins button after hearing that the Twins were upset because he predicted a Dodger sweep. With him is Don Drysdale, who would pitch the series opener. (AP Photo)

10. (*above*) Wearing one of the sombreros that became a lucky talisman for the Dodgers' 1966 pennant run, Al Ferrara congratulates Sandy Koufax (*center*) on his twentieth win of the season. Teammate John Kennedy joins them in presenting Koufax with an oversized baseball in honor of the occasion. (AP Photo)

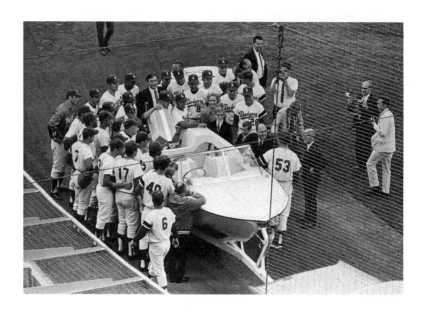

11. In 1968 as Buzzie Bavasi left the Dodgers for San Diego, the players themselves presented him with the parting gift of a boat. Their genuine affection for Bavasi is visible in the gift and the looks of the players. Al Ferrara is in a suit, directly behind the boat, and standing next to his mother is a young Bob Bavasi, wearing glasses. Bob Bavasi remembers seeing a boat hauled from behind the garage door in the outfield. "I heard Don Drysdale say that it was for us from the players. I was at the time, and remain to this day, struck by their overwhelming generosity." (Sporting News/Getty Images)

12. In 1969 Buzzie Bavasi launched the
expansion San Diego Padres as team
president and minority owner. He signed
Al Ferrara to the team, and the Bull hit
fourteen home runs. Here the hopelessness
of an expansion team's first year is
captured by the Bull's bemused gesture as
he sits on home plate. Preston Gomez is
the manager and Ed Vargo the umpire.
(Noel Janko/Bavasi Family Archives)

13. In July 2016 Al Ferrara acknowledges the cheers at Dodger Stadium during the Dodgers Old-Timers Game. (Photo by Chris Williams/ Icon Sportswire; Icon Sportswire via AP Images)

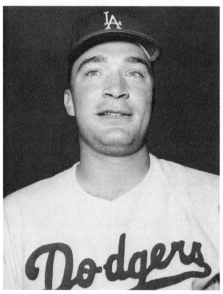

14. Ferrara's teammates cherished his sense of humor and support. He always gave 100 percent on the field and in the clubhouse. (Los Angeles Dodgers)

15. Buzzie Bavasi throws out the ceremonial first pitch during the Padres Opening Day festivities in 2003. Twice nominated for baseball's Hall of Fame, Bavasi led the Dodgers to four world championships between 1955 and 1965. In the over half century since, they have won just two more. (Bavasi Family Archives)

16. Today Al Ferrara devotes much of his time to LA Reads, a Los Angeles Dodgers Foundation partnership with the Los Angeles Public Library that encourages children to read and build a lifelong love of reading. (Photo courtesy of the Los Angeles Public Library)

July   6

Throughout the spring of 1965 the American civil rights movement was engaged in a difficult struggle toward progress. The
march on Selma, Alabama, which culminated in "Bloody Sunday," put pressure on Congress to approve the Voting Rights Act
in August. That same month in the city of Los Angeles tensions
between the African American community and the local police
were building. The black population of Los Angeles embodied
Ralph Ellison's metaphor of the invisible man and woman. The
world of Watts and black Los Angeles was almost never reported
in the pages of the major metropolitan newspapers before 1965.
Indeed the *Los Angeles Times* had no black reporters on its staff
in 1965. The issue of black invisibility in the city was noted by
Dr. Martin Luther King as he wrote about touring Watts in the
days following the bloody August conflagration that was to come
that summer. He encountered a group of young men shouting,
"We won! We won!" King asked them, "How can you say you won
when thirty-four Negroes are dead, your community is destroyed,
and whites are using the riot as an excuse for inaction?" The
response was shouted back immediately: "We won because we
made them pay attention to us." One place in Los Angeles where
people of color were not invisible was on the Los Angeles Dodgers. It was a hallmark of the team's history, and the summer of
1965 called back for Buzzie Bavasi his own pivotal role in deseg-
regating Major League Baseball. That had unfolded nineteen
years earlier in Nashua, New Hampshire.

In the fall of 1945 Branch Rickey, then president and GM of the Brooklyn Dodgers, conducted interviews with several African American ballplayers, determined to find the right man to break baseball's color line. On October 17 he spoke with Roy Campanella for four hours. He had done his research about the power-hitting catcher, son of an Italian father and African American mother. Campanella was impressed with the depth of Rickey's knowledge of his career, but when Rickey asked if he'd like to play for the Dodgers, Campy mistakenly thought he was referring to a Negro League team that Rickey was supposedly going to launch. As one of the highest-paid players in the current Negro League, Campy turned down the offer. A week later Rickey announced the signing of Jackie Robinson, sending him to the Royals, the Dodgers' Triple A Club in Montreal. Campanella said much later, "I could have given myself a swift kick." Rickey also interviewed Don Newcombe, who was playing for the Negro League's Newark Eagles. Rickey and the Dodgers were preparing to launch baseball's great experiment, and Buzzie Bavasi would play an integral role.

Buzzie had returned from World War II ready for a long vacation. He and Evit had planned to live for six months in Sea Island, Georgia, trying to find rest and renewal after three years of combat service. But after just a month Branch Rickey called him and asked him to find a location for a Dodgers' Class B Minor League team in the New England League. Buzzie knew "something was up" and reported for duty. Rickey informed him that he was going to be in charge of the club that would integrate organized (i.e., white) baseball alongside Robinson's experience in Montreal. Rickey was going to sign Newcombe and Campanella and wanted Bavasi to identify a community that would be welcoming. Bavasi looked for a place with a large French Canadian population and a progressive newspaper. He selected Nashua, New Hampshire. Buzzie arrived in Nashua and started laying the groundwork for his effort. As an initial step Bavasi named Fred Dobens, the *Nashua Telegraph*'s managing editor, to be president of the club. That way the city's newspaper would back the

Dodgers' effort. He reached out to the community's large French Canadian population by announcing that the first player on the roster would be Montreal resident Larry Shephard. He further ingratiated himself to the town when he promised an unusual giveaway: each time a Nashua player hit a home run in 1946, local poultry farmer Jack Fallgren would present that player with one hundred baby chicks. The chicks were valued at a total of seventeen dollars, but Roy Campanella pointed out a catch: "It was practically impossible to hit one over the fence because the outfield stretched nearly to the horizon."

Bavasi also launched a Knot-Hole Club, offering discounted tickets to schoolchildren. And he employed Dodgers scout Clyde Sukeforth, who had scouted Jackie Robinson, Don Newcombe, and Roy Campanella, as the head of the Dodgers' baseball school in Nashua. Sukeforth was a Maine native who had played on the 1926 Nashua Millionaires during his Minor League career. But the *Telegraph* article announcing Sukeforth's hiring made no mention that he had scouted Newcombe and Campanella; the Dodgers had not yet announced they were coming to play for Nashua. On April 4, 1946, the Dodgers finally announced that Newcombe and Campanella would play for the team. The two worked out at a New York City YMCA while most of the team trained in North Carolina. Buzzie had not yet picked a manager for the team. He wanted to find someone with experience, and he settled on a thirty-four-year-old former ballplayer who had managed in Trenton for two years. He was about to abandon baseball to teach high school, but when Bavasi offered him the job, he accepted. Walter Alston, who would later end up managing the Major League Dodgers for over twenty years, was on board.

On April 22 Newcombe arrived in town and was followed the next day by Campanella. They had anticipated finding prejudice but were pleasantly surprised by their first meal at the Howard Johnson's Grill. Newcombe said, "There wasn't any name calling; there wasn't any, 'You have to go in the back door. . . .' We sat down and ate in this restaurant and nobody said anything. Roy said, 'Hey, Newk, this town may be all right.'"

When the 1946 season started, Don Newcombe and Roy Campanella became the first black battery in what had been white organized baseball. Campanella started the season by going 3 for 4, with an inside-the-park home run. Two days later Newcombe threw a seven-hit shutout. Both men were off to splendid seasons. Buzzie Bavasi and Branch Rickey went into the season certain of Campanella's and Newcombe's baseball abilities. However, they not sure whether the town would turn out for games featuring an integrated team. Before the season began, Rickey was concerned that the townspeople might boycott the team. Crowds were smaller than expected at the start of the season, and the team lost $18,000 during May. But thanks to Bavasi's judicious engagement with the town of Nashua, attendance turned around. By the end of the season Nashua attendance reached as high as three thousand fans per game.

If the great experiment ran fairly smoothly within Nashua and its clubhouse, Newcombe and Campanella experienced overt racism in other settings, including on the field. The Lynn Red Sox manager, Thomas "Pip" Kennedy, stood in the third base coaching box (typical of Minor League managers) and hurled racial epithets at the two. Newcombe and Campanella were bound by the agreement Branch Rickey had struck with them (as well as with Jackie Robinson) to not retaliate against the racial slurs they would encounter. But Buzzie wasn't part of that agreement, and he felt compelled to respond. He and Walter Alston marched up to Kennedy in the stadium parking lot. Buzzie recalls: "I was going to belt him, knowing, of course, that Alston was right behind me. (Just to make sure, though, I kept turning around to check.) Alston could take on a whole ball club; he was that kind of a man." Bavasi approached the Red Sox bus and told Kennedy, "Why don't you say to me right now what you said to them and I'll kick your fanny. Go ahead and say that to me. I'll take you on." Bavasi looked at the whole Lynn team on the bus: "It was the first time in my life I had ever challenged anybody, and here I was challenging an entire baseball team." Kennedy backed down.

Campanella and Newcombe led Nashua to a triumphant season as New England League champions. Newcombe won fourteen games, and Campanella was named the league's Most Valuable Player. More important, the community had embraced them. Scott Roper quotes a *Telegraph* writer: "Right now, as a matter of fact, they just about own the town and are the two most popular members of the Nashua team." Don Newcombe became a lifelong friend of both Buzzie and Evit; Newk named his daughter Evit. He told Peter Bavasi years later, "Buzzie fought to get Campy and me a job on the Nashua club. He gave us a chance to start a life and a career. He was always in my corner, loaned me money, gave me his car; he looked after me, treated me with great kindness. Besides giving me my first playing job, he gave me my first office job with the Dodgers when my career was over. Buzz was a great influence in my life. He was like my second father. I loved that man."

Buzzie had effectively led a significant part of the integration of professional baseball. He had managed the team's relationship with the town, had found the right manager for the situation, and had personally stood up to racism. Bavasi was grateful to the town of Nashua for its support, and in a letter to Roper he wrote, "I believe that the city of Nashua had a great deal to do with the way other cities handled the racial problem. Had Nashua not accepted Roy and Don with open arms, who knows what might have happened elsewhere(?) [I] think baseball owes a debt of gratitude to the folks in Nashua."

The Los Angeles Dodgers of 1965 carried the legacy of Jackie Robinson and the great experiment. While in 1965 a team like the Boston Red Sox had just two black players on its roster, the Dodgers featured African American stars like Tommy Davis, Willie Davis, John Roseboro, and Jim Gilliam. Lou Johnson had actually played in the Negro Leagues; he was on the 1954 Kansas City Monarchs, managed by Buck O'Neil (and had played alongside the ageless Satchel Paige). That summer the pioneering efforts of Jackie Robinson and the Dodgers eighteen years earlier were once again front and center on the national stage:

on July 6, 1965, House debate began in Washington DC on H.R. 6400—the Civil Rights Act.

While these political and social events were unfolding across America, in Spokane, Washington, the Bull was struggling to find himself. When Ferrara reported to Spokane and played the night after his demotion, he earned the respect of Buzzie Bavasi. He also earned the respect of the new Spokane Indians manager, Duke Snider. Snider was, of course, a legendary Dodger outfielder. As a manager, he shared a conviction that many superstars brought to managing: "I could have made that play; why couldn't you?" Ferrara remembers Snider's frustration as outfielders failed to make a catch that Snider thought they should have made: "He couldn't understand why you couldn't make a play that he [had] made. He was one of the greatest players I ever saw. He couldn't understand why that ball would go off the edge of your glove. He would have caught it. Well, he was Duke Snider. Of course he could have made the catch. He couldn't understand why someone else couldn't do it too."

Al Ferrara had experienced the worst days of his baseball career. He had been living his childhood dream, and now he had been thrown out of the world of his teammates and friends, out of his Casbah, out of the baseball team he had fought to be part of. He was alone, and his family was on the other side of the country. Who could he call? Not his father. It was at moments like these that the loss of his mother—the person who was endlessly loving and forgiving, the woman who could patch up any problem and restore equilibrium to a family—felt devastating. But the Bull showed up. He played. He never complained. He always gave 100 percent on the field. His hand had never healed from the injury in Los Angeles, but he continued to play. After the lights at the ballpark were shut off, he sought solace. He found it in a bar in Spokane. Ferrara was sitting on a stool when a stranger approached and said, "Stop looking at my girl." Ferrara replied he didn't even know who the man's girlfriend was. At that point the stranger put his hand on the Bull's shoulder, and Ferrara punched him. Al summarizes: "So the guy sues me; that's in the LA paper. This is within the space of a week I've destroyed part of my life." Ferrara avoided any legal ramifications, but his hand continued to hurt him. An X-ray was taken, and doctors discovered a fracture that had probably occurred when Al was diving for a ball back in Los Angeles. He had to sit out for ten days while he healed.

The Bull, as always, found the edge of life and teetered on it precariously. That hard wiring within him offered the Bull a long string of experiences that most people have perhaps once in a lifetime. For instance, one time he came back to an Arizona hotel with two female wrestlers. Another time he made love on the mud floor of a hut in the jungles of Venezuela.

In 1962 Ferrara had been dispatched to winter ball in Caracas, where fans are violently passionate about the game. In the dugout at games soldiers would stand guard in full military uniform, carrying machine guns. The Bull was rooming with Monk Williams in a hotel and became friendly with the maid. There was a language barrier, but she told Ferrara where she lived. It was apparently in a distant village, who knows where. Monk argued against Al's making a journey to this village. Who knew what he'd find there? Was this a setup? There was a language barrier, so at best there was the possibility for endless confusion and Al's getting lost somewhere in the jungle. The Bull brushed that all off, hailed a cab, and gave the driver the address. The driver balked, but Ferrara insisted, and he was driven far out into the hinterlands. The cab arrived at a collection of huts. Ferrara told the driver to come back in an hour, and the driver seemed happy to race off. Al recaps: "I went into what is a teepee, okay? It was just a dirt floor. And she had a mattress on the ground." The Bull was alone with the maid in a remote environment, a place where he had no idea what to expect. But he had sought out the adventure and found it satisfying.

The cab returned and drove Ferrara back to Caracas. The team had done well and was in the playoffs. The night before the first postseason game there was a party, and naturally Ferrara was there. He had been pursuing a Dutch stewardess, and the mood of the party was relaxed. He took off his shoes, drinking, chatting up the flight attendant—and stepped on a broken bottle. He cut the bottom of his foot badly. A teammate, dubbed "Camilio Chief" because of his native heritage, was also at the party, and he took the Bull to the hospital. The cut was stitched up, but it was clear there was no way Ferrara could play in the next day's playoff game. He realized he needed to get out of Caracas; the fans would not be happy to lose one of the better power hitters on the team. So Al and the Chief make arrangements to get a flight. When they arrived at the airport, the Chief pushed Ferrara in a wheel chair through the parking lot to the terminal. Half a dozen fans had somehow heard about the accident and were there. Al recalls: "They're screaming at me, trying to challenge me in Spanish, yelling at me. The Chief is running down the runway to get me onto the plane, and they're yelling from the back—Ferrara!!" Al barely made it onto the plane under a barrage of verbal abuse and got back to the relative safety of New York.

Consider another offseason, this one in the Arizona Instructional League. In batting practice one day Ferrara swung hard and tore tendons in his left hand. He was put in the hospital and then sent home to New York. That injury nagged at him his entire career. He went back to his old neighborhood friends: Bobby "Weese," a.k.a. Bobby Genovese; Marvin the Clown, a kid with enormous ears; Black Eddy; Flyshitnose; Bobby T (Bobby Tarzia), who would later move to Los Angeles and start a hair salon as Mr. Robert; and Johnny Nippo. Johnny Nippo held regular card games at his home in Brooklyn. One evening during a card game there was a knock on Nippo's door. Ferrara opened it to reveal two guys with shotguns. They ordered the players up against the wall. The gunmen ordered them to take off their pants. All of the participants took off their pants and threw them on the floor. The thieves scooped up the pants with the cash inside them and took off. After they left, the Bull said, "Usually you lose your shirt; this time we lost our pants." It was a cold walk back home through the December streets of Brooklyn with Al wearing just his shorts.

Consider the winter of 1963, when Ferrara was in Puerto Rico playing winter ball. As Christmas approached, he told Dodger executive Al Campanis that he was going to fly back to New York to visit his family. He'd miss four or five days of practice. Campanis replied that he couldn't allow that: "When guys leave here, they never come back. If you go, you'll be suspended from the Puerto Rican League." Ferrara responded, "You can't tell me that. If I want to fly back there, I'll pay my own way." At the time his cash reserve was, to say the least, low, as Al confesses: "I ain't got two cents in my pocket. But I said, 'I'll pay my own way.'" Campanis reiterated that the league would suspend him. Ferrara walked out of his office and decided there was only one man he could call to get the money for the flight: Buzzie Bavasi.

Ferrara made the call: "Buzzie, I want to go back to see my child and my wife. And I don't have the money for the plane ticket." Buzzie was surprised to hear this. "You just got your World Series check a couple of months ago," he said. The Bull replied with an accounting of Ferraranomics: "Well, I gave some of it away. My grandmother got $500. I had to send some money home. And the crap tables here in Puerto Rico got the rest." Buzzie asked what else the Bull had been doing. Ferrara said he'd gone to the shows at the big clubs and seen Sophie Tucker. "Sophie Tucker!" Buzzie exclaimed. "You make sure you say hello to Sophie Tucker for me." From his years in New York Buzzie had befriended many show business people, Sophie Tucker being one of them. Invoking the name of Sophie Tucker seemed to turn the key to the cashbox: "I'll send you $300," Bavasi said.

Having received the cash via wire, Ferrara made his usual well-reasoned decision about the immediate disposition of the money: "I hadda take one last shot. I took the three hundred to the crap table—and blew it." Now he was really concerned. Somehow he had to get back to New York. He called up his old friend Bobby "Weese" Genovese. He specified to Bobby to arrange things in this way: if Weese sent the Bull the money, Al knew himself well enough to realize he'd blow it at the tables. Weese needed to purchase a prepaid ticket; it was the only way the $300 wouldn't go down the sinkhole. Bobby made the arrangement, the prepaid ticket was at the airport, the Bull went back to New York, and Buzzie's $300 was out the window. As Campanis predicted, Ferrara was indeed suspended from the Puerto Rican League and never went back. Living on the edge. Nerves of steel.

Now it was late June 1965. The Bull had been demoted to Spokane and was sitting out for ten days. Neither Ferrara nor the Spokane team was doing well.

A frustrated Duke Snider took Ferrara aside and told him that he was wasting his talent; he wasn't playing the way he was capable. The Bull explained about his hand injury, and Snider told him to take a sponge and put it at the end of the bat. Then they started talking about hitting. Snider asked him what Ferrara was doing when he got up to the plate, and the Bull told him about all the adjustments he had made as he advanced up to the Major Leagues: his timing mechanisms, his strategy of "zoning" pitches (attacking the ball in selected zones and letting pitches not in those zones go by), etc. Snider replied with the wisdom of the natural athlete: "You ain't doing jack. If you ain't playing well here, you ain't going back to the big league. Don't think about nothing. Go up there and just swing the bat; you've got nothing to lose." Ferrara said he would try this zen exercise: he would think about thinking about nothing. He had a challenge in doing this: Ferrara was a "quiet" hitter—that is, in the batter's box he stood still; he didn't have a tic or a trigger, a giveaway movement he made before swinging. In order to get his mind off of running through the mechanical pointers that he used to assemble his swing, he decided to pump his bat. He would pump before swinging as a technique to get his mind off his thoughts and let his swing become more instinctual. He explains: "I just kept pumping; nothing was going on in my mind, and I would pump and pump and pump, and then as the pitcher was releasing the ball, I would swing the bat, and I started whacking the ball." Ferrara was reacting to the ball, and he kept that pumping movement for the rest of his career. Years later, when his friend Don Zimmer was managing the Cubs, Zim introduced the Bull to the great Cubs star Andre Dawson. Dawson immediately was able to do an impression of Ferrara at the plate, pumping the bat.

If we accept F. Scott Fitzgerald's assessment of intelligence as one's ability to hold two opposed ideas in the mind at the same time and still retain the ability to function, that describes the mental condition of the average professional baseball player. On the one hand, players make mechanical adjustments as they climb up each step of the baseball ladder. Pitchers discover a weak spot in the swing; the player makes an adjustment to meet that challenge. On the other hand, a hitter can't be thinking too much as he bats. Once a pitcher throws a fastball to home plate, the batter has only four-tenths of one second to respond. In that less than a half-second the batter has to decide whether to swing and has to make other choices as well—for example, to go with the pitch or pull it or how to best hit to the right side of the infield if there is a runner on second. There are a thousand calculations that must be made in that four-tenths of a second. Of course a batter cannot actually let his mind move through all of those possibilities but must rather let instinct take over. The superstars, the naturals in the game—Willie Mays, Hank Aaron, Duke Snider—are purely instinctual players. But those like Al Ferrara, the ones who battle their way to the big leagues through endless practice and adjustment and a honing of their skills, are continually engaged in the zen exercise of learning a technique only to purposefully clear their minds of what they have learned once they are at the plate.

The Bull had experienced multiple examples of this dichotomy. In the Minor Leagues Ferrara quickly realized that pitchers got ahead in the count by throwing fastballs and that Minor League umpires tended to call high strikes. So for his time in the Minors he had to learn how to hit high fastballs. But when he got to the Major Leagues in 1963, he saw that big league umpires would call strikes down at the knees; everything Major League pitchers threw tended to be down. The umpires wouldn't call a high strike. Al says: "In the Minor Leagues [a high fastball] was a strike, and I had to swing at it, but in the Major Leagues it was a ball." So now Ferrara had to learn *not* to swing at those high pitches. He wanted to school himself to stand at the plate and take high pitches. But what coach or pitcher would spend time throwing balls to someone who just stood there? Ferrara waited until practice was over. Then he would set up the pitching machine and would walk up in the batter's box so that the balls would come in high. And he would hold up on swinging. He'd practice taking the high pitch between five hundred and a thousand times a day so that when he saw a high pitch, he would not swing at it but take the pitch. He concludes: "I wasn't learning to swing; I was learning what *not* to swing at."

In today's baseball world young children have expert coaching from an extremely early age. Baseball camps abound with former big league players setting nine-year-olds up with proper batting mechanics. The Bull himself now conducts Dodger baseball camps and coaches grade school children, marveling at their beautiful swings. As Ferrara grew up, there was no coach to offer instruction at all. Each kid developed his own batting stance, often by imitating the Major Leaguer he most admired. It wasn't until the Bull reached the highest levels of professional baseball—nearly at the Major Leagues—that Ferrara connected with a coach who offered significant technical advice: Kenny Myers.

Kenny Myers was a revolutionary baseball coach. Signed as a player by the Cardinals during World War II, when he was only fifteen, he suffered an injury and never made it to the Majors. But he was an inveterate student of the game and a compulsive inventor of baseball training devices (and, like so many characters in the Dodger constellation, a cigar perpetually dangled from his lips). He was a short, stubby man, and he smoked a short, stubby cigar—the old De Nobili brand, smoked with relish by Italian Americans and known by non-Italians as "stinkers." Collegiate baseball coach John Herbold credits Myers with inventing soft toss and recalls seeing Myers in the 1950s soft-tossing baseballs to Gil Hodges almost head on. Myers invented a pop-up batting tee and taught hitting using devices such as a bat with a crooked handle (it proved that hitters don't roll their wrists when they hit the ball but rather after); a batting net (he called it the "Bat Rite"—imagine a bat with a rectangular frame in its sweet spot, in which a hitter would catch the pitch if he swung properly); and the half-bat–half-tennis racket. He would throw basketballs to players to hit, causing one veteran scout to ask in spring training, "Who the hell is that maniac throwing basketballs to Frank Howard?" There was a scientific logic to the exercise: if a player hit a basketball with a baseball bat, it would hurt unless he hit the ball on the sweet spot of the bat. Myers was perhaps most famous for discovering the speedy Willie Davis while he was running track in Los Angeles, teaching him how to hit a baseball, and transforming him into a Major League outfielder. His eccentric teaching tools were held at arm's length by conservative baseball old timers, but when the Bull first encountered Myers in the Arizona Instructional League, he embraced the short man with the cigar glued to the side of his mouth.

At that point early in his career Ferrara considered that he had an average arm at best. But Myers said to him, "You don't have an average arm. You have an outstanding arm. You just don't know how to throw. You don't know how to approach the ball." The next day Myers took Ferrara to the outfield and worked with him on how to approach the ball. He taught Ferrara to charge the ball, pick it up, and let it go. As Myers said, "If you play the game not to lose, you ain't going no place. If you catch the ball and throw a guy out at the plate, you've done something." At first the Bull's throws sailed all over the field. He admits, "Everybody would laugh." But the next year in spring training Ferrara remembers his fellow Minor Leaguers seeing him throw and then jumping up and down in celebration. From that point on the Bull believed what had Myers told him: he had a great arm. He considered it one of his assets.

Myers talked baseball wherever he was, and that was frequently in a bar. In the Arizona Instructional League the entertainment options following a day at the ballpark consisted of either the dog track or a bar. Baseball players tended toward the bar since there were women there, although as Ferrara notes, "At two o'clock in the morning you're not going to run into Miss America."

The Bull and Myers often adjourned from the field to the bar, and there Myers continued to talk about hitting. The conversation segued into base running. Ferrara mentioned that when he slid, he put his hand down and frequently hurt it. Myers immediately responded: "What are you worrying about? I'll show you how to slide." The dance floor was filled with people. But Myers, without missing a beat, took his drink, held it up in his right hand, moved onto the dance floor, and executed a slide without spilling a drop. "Okay, Bull, now you do it," he instructed. So Ferrara took his scotch and water out on the dance floor, slid—and didn't spill a drop. He learned the art of sliding in a bar. Kenny Myers would reappear in the Bull's life during the tumultuous summer of 1965 and once again throw him a lifeline with the confidence of a man who teaches sliding on the dance floor of an Arizona bar.

Back in Los Angeles Buzzie Bavasi opened his *Los Angeles Times* on July 1, 1965, to find the great sports columnist Jim Murray had written about a fictional phone call he made to Bavasi: "Listen, Buzzie. You know the stories going around about your team? You know, watching the Dodgers bat is like listening to a silent movie . . . To speed up baseball . . . just have the Dodgers sign for three outs every inning and get on with it." Then he offers a suggestion for the team's lack of hitting: "Gil Hodges at Washington owes you a favor or two. Right? Now, Buzzie, copy this name down. They've got a guy over there I swear could hit a ball farther than any guy I've ever seen. A big guy. . . ." Yes, Murray's satiric suggestion was to trade for Frank Howard. The Dodgers started July in first place, but how long could they hold on with an anemic offense? A team based on nerves of steel also asks its fans to possess nerves of steel. It's easier to be a fan of the Bronx Bombers than the masters of the 1–0 win.

Away from Elysian Park (the location of Dodger Stadium), greater anxieties continued to surface in Los Angeles. On July 10 the city's Board of Rights heard charges of bigotry regarding suspended police officer Michael B. Hannon. Hannon—described in the *Los Angeles Times* as "blond," was charged with conduct unbecoming a police officer because of his participation in pro–civil rights demonstrations. Police officers called as witnesses described seeing Hannon picketing, singing, and carrying a placard along with other demonstrators as the Congress of Racial Equality demonstrated against a White Citizens' Council meeting. The significance of this reporting is in the invisibility of citizens of color: when a white police officer demonstrated against a bigoted group, that drew attention. For the black protestors there was silence.

Los Angeles seems to breed a certain self-satisfied myopia about itself. Perhaps it is the film industry, with its pressure to enlarge one's sense of oneself, that permeates through an entire city's psyche. LA regularly cycles through periods of congratulating itself as an open and welcoming city to those of all racial backgrounds and then suddenly exploding in racial frustration and uprising. The 1992 riots that followed the Rodney King beating took the city by surprise, and yet uprisings had occurred before, none larger than the Watts Rebellion of 1965.

During the Great Migration, when millions of African American families moved from the south to urban centers such as New York, Chicago, and Los Angeles, LA was perceived as open, sunny, and less racist than other big American cities. The reality is that early on, even before the great push of people into Southern California during World War II to work at the Boeing and Lockheed plants that were churning out airplanes, restricted housing covenants were in place throughout Los Angeles. As early as 1910, 80 percent of the city was off limits to people of color, and by the 1940s that figure had grown to nearly 95 percent. African Americans and Mexican Americans who sought housing after serving in World War II or being employed in the defense industry during the war found their options limited to East and South Los Angeles. The result was that housing in those locales became scarce and offered real estate developers the chance to cash in on undeveloped land in places like Compton. Real estate speculators used racial animus to their financial advantage in a practice known as "block busting": a speculator would buy a house in an all-white neighborhood and then rent it to a black family. White neighbors would flee the area in panic; the speculator would pick up those homes for a highly discounted price and then sell them to black families for a profit.

In 1963 African American state legislator William Byron Rumford drafted a bill to block housing discrimination in the state of California. It was signed into law in 1963. The next year the California Real Estate Association launched a ballot initiative that was labeled Proposition 14. It was an amendment to the state constitution, and its goal was to overturn the Rumford Fair Housing Act and enshrine the legality of discrimination: "Neither the State nor any subdivision or agency thereof shall deny, limit or abridge, directly or indirectly, the right of any person, who is willing or desires to sell, lease or rent any part or all of his real property, to decline to sell, lease or rent such property to such person or persons as he, in his absolute discretion, chooses." The petition to add the proposition to the ballot gathered over one million signatures, and it was placed on the November ballot. The *Los Angeles Times* endorsed Proposition 14, but it was bitterly opposed by Governor Edmund Brown and the California attorney general, Stanley Mosk. Mosk said, "It sugar-coats bigotry with an appeal to generalities we can accept, while ignoring the specific problem that confronts us." Brown was more forceful, drawing a comparison of the campaign for the proposition to "another hate binge which began more than 30 years ago in a Munich beer hall." Their words fell on deaf ears. In November, 1964, Proposition 14 passed with 65 percent approval. Over two-thirds of Los Angeles County voted in favor of the measure. Within months the federal government cut off housing funds to the state. The constitutionality of the measure was challenged, and ultimately in 1966 the California Supreme Court held that Proposition 14 violated the federal Constitution's equal protection clause and ruled it unconstitutional. The U.S. Supreme Court upheld that decision a year later. Governor Brown may have paid a price for his strong stance against racial discrimination. In 1966 he was defeated for reelection by Ronald Reagan, who opposed the Rumford Act (calling it an attempt to "give one segment of our population a right at the expense of the basic rights of all our citizens"). It should be noted that Reagan also opposed Proposition 14 as "not a wise measure," but maybe by opposing the Rumford Act, he had made his basic position clear.

In the summer of 1965, however, Proposition 14 was the law of the land. And the man in charge of law enforcement in Los Angeles was Police Chief William Parker. He had inherited a highly corrupt force when he was sworn in in 1950 (think of Raymond Chandler's picture of Los Angeles cops) and was credited with professionalizing the force into the *"Dragnet"* image it projected on national television. But to the black and Latino communities in Los Angeles the police represented an authority that regularly engaged in brutality. That brutality was as invisible to the general white public as was the community of color.

The Dodgers held a unique position in this complex mix of racial discrimination, hostility, and volatility. They were proud pioneers in equality and continued that tradition with community leaders like revered alums Jackie Robinson and Don Newcombe and current players like Maury Wills, who owned a business in South Central, and John Roseboro, who lived in Compton. The general population of Los Angeles may have been floating on a bubble of myopia in the summer of 1965, but Wills, Roseboro, and Tommy Davis knew better. Within six weeks that illusion would burst into flames.

On July 5 the Dodgers were in Cincinnati, and they played an ugly game. They committed two errors, lost two leads, and ultimately lost the game and first place to the Reds. After the game Walter Alston held a team meeting behind closed doors and delivered a blistering tongue-lashing. Coach Danny Ozark said afterward, "We needed something like that to loosen us up." Although it's always difficult to quantify the positive effects of vitriol, the next day the Dodgers scored eleven runs and returned to first place. Their road trip took them to Pittsburgh, and then the All-Star break gave most of the team a breather, although Koufax, Drysdale, and Wills played in the game. Following the All-Star Game, the Dodgers went on a winning streak at home, and by July 20 they were comfortably again in first place, leading Cincinnati by three and a half games. While they lost some ground at the end of the month, July 1965 ended with the Dodgers in first place by a single game. But August was around the corner.

August   7

Before he reported promptly to Spokane, the Bull had pulled up stakes from the Mayfair Hotel and bid an abrupt good-bye to his beloved Casbah. A professional baseball player's life is itinerant on two levels. Working his way through the Minor Leagues, a player moves from town to town each year and not infrequently moves twice within a year. In addition, during the long baseball season players spend half of their time on the road. So they experience dislocation annually on a macro level and also from week to week on a micro level. Even after they reach the Major Leagues, the journey is not settled. Players can be traded; they can be sent back down to the Minor Leagues; they can be released. All of those life-changing occurrences may happen in a shocking twenty-four-hour period. How do ballplayers maintain any kind of equanimity during such upheavals, especially when their jobs are inherently full of the pressure to block out distractions and focus strictly on succeeding on the field? Added to such difficulties is the pressure for the player who is not a star, the man who has to fight for a place on the roster, as Ferrara did. Al states: "Look, I was always fighting for a position, always fighting to stay where I was. There was somebody on my back because I had passed a lot of guys up; a lot of guys were now coming after me. If you want to hold that position, there's a lot of pressure." How does a player handle the pressure of a vagabond life coupled with the pressure of fighting for a job?

In Ferrara's case the Bull had an innate ability to follow an old Cherokee proverb and not "let yesterday use up too much of today." Wiping his hands clean, moving on, acknowledging his mistakes but not dwelling on them—the Bull had lived his life in the moment, embracing wherever he found himself with no regrets. Ferraranomics is built on this principle. Peter Bavasi, who would later work with his father in the San Diego Padre front office, remembers the day Buzzie asked Ferrara to come up to the area where players received mail. There was a shelf with pigeon holes to collect items that arrived for Dodger players. Each player had a couple of letters in his pigeon hole—except for the Bull. Ferrara's mail filled his slot and spilled over into a box below the shelf. All those letters were bills—unpaid bills. Buzzie instructed Peter to have the Bull do something about the situation. Ferrara dutifully looked at the box of overdue bills and said cheerfully, "I'll take care of this." He pulled a trash can over and started tossing bills into the trash.

"Wait a second," objected Peter. "What are you doing?"

"I'm taking care of this," the Bull replied. He glanced at each envelope and kept tossing them into the waste basket. Occasionally he would set one aside. He threw away every bill that wasn't marked "FINAL NOTICE." Then he explained his technique: "See, here are the bills marked 'FINAL NOTICE.' These I'll open. All the others can wait." He had final notice bills from the Diners Club, American Express, and the May Company department store. The expanded availability of credit cards during the 1960s had greatly accelerated Ferraranomics. Al applied—and was accepted—for multiple credit cards, and when he happily reached his limit on one, he was able to turn to the next card to "Open Sesame" for purchases.

Al explained to Peter: "Okay. Diners Club—owe them $560. I'll send them sixty dollars. They get some money, the restaurants I ate at already got their money—everybody's happy." He repeated the process with American Express and the May Company, paying off $50 on a $700 bill and $35 on a $400 bill. His theory was to creatively support the American economy by spreading a little wealth to restaurants and stores via his credit card expenditures: "The stores are happy; they got their money; the credit card company gets some money; everyone is happy." The trash can stuffed with unpaid bills gets emptied, and everyone wins.

The Bull's instinct to make everyone around him profitable and happy extended to his many relationships with women. He may have dated women in every town to which his baseball career sent him, and they included a vast spectrum of American society—from the strippers at the El Rancho to the baseball Annies who traveled from out of town and somehow magically knew the hotels at which the team was staying—and Ferrara's approach was to share joy with all of them. Living on the edge also meant living in the moment. He effectively brushed aside worries about the future and dismissed regrets from the past and was able to make the most of what he was experiencing right there and then.

In Spokane during the August 1965 the Bull was applying this philosophy of not letting yesterday take up too much of today to his hitting. As per Duke Snider's advice, he was clearing his head of thoughts, stepping into the batter's box, and just reacting to the pitch. It was working. He was crushing doubles off the wall, and the home runs were starting to add up.

Back in Los Angeles after the first ten days of August, the Dodgers remained in first place—barely. The Giants had climbed to just a game behind them, and Cincinnati and Milwaukee were just two games behind. The team's nerves-of-steel pitching and offense continued to win close games, and many of the wins were fueled by the remarkable Maury Wills. The Bull firmly believes that Wills was the most dominant player in baseball during the 1960s. He expounds: "Think about what I'm saying—in an era with Willie Mays and Hank Aaron and Mickey Mantle, I think Maury Wills was the greatest offensive player of his time. He was the catalyst for four World Series teams." Before each game Wills would bandage his wounded legs, like a warrior preparing to go into battle. Whenever Wills got on base, Dodger Stadium would resound with the fans chanting, "Go! Go! Go!" As of August 10 it appeared as though Wills could break his own stolen base record of 104, set in 1962. But he paid a price: his game was based on speed, on his legs, and they took a terrible beating. All the sliding he did produced cuts and bruises and strawberries up and down his legs. After games Wills would slowly strip off his uniform, revealing legs that were battered and often bloody. He would sit for nearly an hour in an ice bath and a whirlpool trying to somehow keep his greatest assets healthy. The baseball season became a brutal marathon, but Wills was a perfectionist, determined to never back down or slow down on the base paths.

On August 10, 1965, the Dodgers were at home and won a typically close game over the Mets, 4–3. Koufax pitched a complete game, striking out fourteen. The next day in South Los Angeles, Marquette Frye, a young black man, was driving with his brother Ronald two blocks from their home. They were at the corner of 116th Street and Avalon Boulevard when Frye was pulled over by a white California highway patrolman. Officer Lee W. Minikus arrested Marquette Frye for driving while intoxicated. Ronald went to their home and retrieved their mother. When Mrs. Frye saw her son being arrested, she objected and then fought with the arresting officers. She tore one man's shirt, and then an officer struck Marquette's head with a nightstick and arrested all three. A crowd had gathered to witness the melee, and anger quickly spread into violence. Frye's arrest prompted an outbreak in Watts that night. Cars were overturned and businesses burned, and the most significant upheaval of the civil rights era began. It was called the Watts Riots or the Watts Rebellion, depending on the prism through which one viewed the event. That night the Dodgers were at home, again playing the Mets. Don Drysdale shut them out, and the Dodgers won in typical fashion, 1–0. They had the next day, August 12, off. That day the Los Angeles County Human Relations Committee called a meeting to try to calm the situation, but it didn't help. Rioting resumed that night, and fires blazed through South Los Angeles. Residents shot at firemen responding to calls, and looting of businesses increased. Lou Johnson lived in South-Central, and so did John Roseboro.

On Friday, August 13, the morning edition of the *Los Angeles*

Times carried a long headline: "New Rioting: Stores Looted, Cars Destroyed. Many Fires Started; 75 Reported Injured in 2nd Violent Night." The Dodgers reported to Elysian Park and played the Pittsburgh Pirates. The starting lineup for the Dodgers included African Americans Maury Wills, Jim Gilliam, Lou Johnson, and Willie Davis. John Roseboro had the night off and spent the game in the left-field bullpen listening to news reports on a transistor radio. The Dodgers won, 3–1, and Roseboro, Johnson, and rookie Willie Crawford drove home together, wearing their Dodger uniforms as a kind of visual cue to the police that they were not rioters. Ron Fairly invited Roseboro and his family to stay with him in the San Fernando Valley during the violence, but Roseboro declined. He was never one to back down from a fight. He sat by the front door of his home with a gun, guarding it successfully. Maury Wills had opened a dry cleaning business with a white partner on Santa Barbara Avenue, a few miles from Watts. Each day during the uprising Wills would spend two or three hours standing in front of Maury Wills Stolen Base Cleaners, a testament to his neighbors that this was a black-owned business. Then he would go to the ballpark and attempt to steal some bases.

The press coverage of what was unfolding castigated the violence, and that attitude bespoke a sort of racial blindness that drifted into the sports pages. The *Los Angeles Times* report on Friday's game included this description: "Willie Davis did the frug, the watusi and the twist in robbing Bob Clemente and Manuel Mota of extra-base hits. . . . The crowd of 32,551 seemed a bit subdued, perhaps because of the smoke that apparently drifted in from the riot area and hung like a pall over the stadium."

By Saturday the death toll had reached eight, and the National Guard was called in. Over the following days as many as fourteen thousand California guard troops mobilized in South Los Angeles. A curfew was set for that night, but the Dodgers' game was played as usual. Sandy Koufax shut out the Pirates over ten innings and then scored the winning run—and the only run of the game—in the bottom of the tenth. Maury Wills did not play, but Gilliam, Davis, and Roseboro did. The *Times* reported with a distinct lack of sensitivity to the underlying situation: "A crowd of 'only' 29,237 fans turned out at Dodger Stadium and the management said the seriousness of the local situation hurt attendance by at least 15,000. . . . Willie Crawford, who resides in the curfew area, spent the night at Johnny Roseboro's home. . . . Walt Alston, Danny Ozark and Trixie Tracewski, who live just west of Crenshaw, had the vicarious thrill of seeing armed national guardsmen patrolling in the area Saturday afternoon."

The rioting continued Saturday night, and by Sunday the death toll had reached twenty-five. The curfew for that night was now set at 8 p.m. The Dodgers were scheduled for an afternoon game as they faced the Pirates in the concluding game of the series. The Dodgers lost, 4–2. Sports columnist Sid Ziff summarized the week as one in which players who lived in South Central worried about how they would get home each night and others rushing after the game to get TV updates.

By Monday, August 16, the headlines reported the rioting was dying down in South-Central and shifting to Long Beach. The Dodgers played that night, losing to Philadelphia. Their lead in the pennant race was down to just half a game. The next day Governor Edmund "Pat" Brown declared that "[The] . . . riot is over." Over the course of the six-day Watts uprising thirty-four people died, one thousand were injured, and almost four thousand were arrested. An official state investigation ultimately found that the conflagration was the result of long-standing inequities in employment, substandard housing, and inadequate schools. Later that fall the *Los Angeles Times* quoted a forty-six-year-old father of six who lived in Watts: "If I ever made enough money, I would move out of Watts like all the other big shots. So I'm here, so what the hell. Los Angeles isn't all it's cracked up to be. Wherever you go, you're black—that's all there is to it."

In 1965 there were no black GMs in baseball. The first African American to serve as a GM was Bill Lucas of the Atlanta Braves. A veteran of Atlanta's organization, he was promoted to handle the responsibilities of a GM on September, 17, 1976—with an asterisk. His official title was vice-president of player personnel, but his duties were those of a GM. It was a difficult situation—tempestuous owner Ted Turner was prone to actions such as naming himself field manager of the team. (After one day of this experiment the National League president ruled that an owner could not manage his own team. Tragically in May 1979 Lucas suffered a cardiac arrest and died at the age of forty-three. The next African American GM was Bob Watson, hired by the Houston Astros after the 1993 season. Forty-six years after Jackie Robinson had integrated the Major Leagues, there was finally a black GM who officially carried the title.)

If players in the Major Leagues constitute a very small club—fewer than twenty thousand men have ever played in a Major League baseball game throughout the league's history—then the club of GMs is infinitesimally small. A team carries a twenty-five-man roster up until September, at which point it expands to forty players (thereby fundamentally changing the nature of a team and the game during the crucial final month of the regular season; it is another anomaly of baseball rules, like the DH; it makes baseball the only professional sport to change its rules from league to league and within the time frame of a season). But if there are twenty-five men on a team during a season, there is only one GM. In 1965 just twenty men in all the world held the job of GM of a Major League team. Several of those men were from baseball families, passing along the family business: Lee MacPhail, GM of Baltimore in 1965, was the son of Larry MacPhail, executive with the Reds, Dodgers, and Yankees (and now Lee's son Andy is president of the Philadelphia Phillies); Chub Feeney was the nephew of Giants' owner Horace Stoneham; Branch Rickey's son followed his father into the upper levels of baseball management.

Indeed the skill set required for a baseball GM of the era before free agency was probably best passed down from father to son or mentor to protégé. Today baseball executives subdivide their duties in line with a corporate structure; before the free-agency era the GM relied on a personal feel for the organization and the people within it. Branch Rickey built his system at the Dodgers with his "out of quantity comes quality" philosophy: he trusted that the sheer number of players in the system would result in excellence rising to the top. One could say his effort to integrate Major League baseball was based at heart in this same philosophy: there was a vast pool of immensely talented players that he sought to join his system. In Vero Beach in the late 1940s there would be up to 650 players in spring training. There were so many numbers to issue to players that they would be printed on pieces of paper and pinned to their uniforms.

Rickey instructed his scouts to look for a few simple criteria. For pitchers: if a kid possessed a Major League fastball, that's all a scout needed to see. Rickey believed a pitching prospect could be taught everything else. For position players: find a player who is great in one of the five basic tools—the ability to hit, hit with power, run, field, and throw. If a player had great natural talent in one of these areas, he could be taught the rest.

Rickey put a premium on speed. Certainly that legacy was apparent in the 1965 Dodgers, fueled by Maury Wills, whom the Bull called the greatest offensive player he ever saw. Speed afoot is one thing that cannot be taught. Beyond speed Rickey next looked for strength of arm, then power, then defense. Last was hitting; of all the skills, he felt that was the most teachable.

A prototype of the Branch Rickey scout was Bob Fontaine Sr. He scouted first for the Brooklyn Dodgers, then followed Rickey to the Pirates in 1951. Buzzie Bavasi hired him to be the San Diego Padres first director of scouting and player development, and Fontaine eventually became the Padres GM. Buzzie's son Bob remembers Fontaine taking him to a high school baseball game to scout some prospects. He walked down the third and first base lines, looking at arm angles. He looked at the pitcher. After about twenty minutes he turned to Bob and said, "Let's go." Bob was startled. Why were they leaving so quickly? Fontaine explained: "I saw the kid throw a Major League fastball, so I know he can do that. We can teach him everything else."

Branch Rickey was famously a Methodist who, as a gesture

to the religiosity of his parents, particularly his mother, didn't believe in playing baseball on Sundays, and he was a great believer in players getting married at an early age. When visiting his father at work, Peter Bavasi remembers frequently encountering Rickey: "He had bushy eyebrows, always wore a three-piece suit, and smoked a cigar." He would tap Peter on the head, and then a gentle shower of cigar ash would fall on Peter's scalp.

Did every American man smoke cigars in the 1950s? It seems as though every Dodger executive and scout did. Walter O'Malley smoked cigars held in custom-made linen cigar holders. When Peter Bavasi became president of the Toronto Blue Jays, O'Malley sent him a letter of congratulations and said he was enclosing a good luck charm. It was one of the linen cigar holders.

All of these lessons were absorbed by Buzzie Bavasi, who then developed his own set of criteria for success. He began with the other baseball GMs. Within this tiny group Buzzie had a golden rule of protocol, quoted by his son Peter (who himself would become GM of the San Diego Padres and president of the Toronto Blue Jays and Cleveland Indians): "Never get into a disagreement with a general manager that can't immediately be repaired. Never hold a grudge; never get anybody mad at you—because there are only nineteen other clubs you can deal with. Anger one guy, and it's not just one club less that you have to deal with; that GM is going to be telling everyone else that you're a jerk, and once that starts, you're going to have a tough time."

This is not to say that GMs cannot be, shall we say, strategic. A legendary story about Buzzie's ability to outmaneuver his opposing GMs involves the military, Willie Mays's generosity toward his mother, and Buzzie's own wartime service. Peter Bavasi actually witnessed the beginning of the story. He was twelve at the time, and Peter accompanied Buzzie to a meeting with Giants GM Chub Feeney at the Biltmore Hotel in New York. Feeney began discussing his great young star Willie Mays. It was 1952; Mays was twenty-one and had won the Rookie of the Year award the previous season. The Korean War had heated up, and there was talk of drafting Mays into the army. Feeney told Bavasi with a chuckle, "We can't afford to lose this guy—he's the sole support of his mother."

Bavasi pulled as much information as he could out of Feeney. Then the next day Buzzie called up a friend with whom he had served in the infantry and asked if he could connect him with the commandant of the army reserves. His friend made the introduction, and Bavasi called him up. He told the commandant how grateful he was for everything the army had taught him; it was difficult, but it was a wonderful way of teaching young people how to be truly American patriots. And he added that he thought it would be a wonderful example for young Americans if Willie Mays of the Giants could serve in the army. The commandant replied that they were working on that very case, but they understood that Mays was the sole support of his mother. Bavasi generously replied that the Brooklyn Dodgers would underwrite the well-being of Mays's mother and take care of all of her expenses. Whatever Willie was doing for her now, the Dodgers would do it even better. Bavasi stressed: "He doesn't have to go overseas; just be on a base in America and then we'll take care of the mother."

Mays spent the whole of the 1953 season in the army—and the Brooklyn Dodgers won the pennant. It was an impressive example of Buzzie Bavasi's powers of persuasion. Buzzie was the acknowledged king of bending the baseball rules to the benefit of the club for which he was working but doing so without ever breaking them. He was amenable to employing players who pushed the envelope of off-the-field behavior in the same way. He said at the end of his career that he had experienced an enormous amount of fun during his career in baseball.

But now it was the middle of August 1965, and smoke from the fires in Watts was hanging over Dodger Stadium. Bavasi was more invested in the American civil rights struggle than any of the other baseball GMs—he had been part of that struggle just eighteen years earlier. That struggle had entered a new and more intense phase. The heroic act of breaking the color line had a relatively simple dynamic; the continuing push toward economic and social justice for all was more complex and disruptive. Buzzie

Bavasi and the Dodgers were now dealing with the pressures of a rift in the social fabric, exposed and bleeding at the same time as they entered the final six weeks of an intense pennant race. There was a fight coming their way.

On August 19 the Dodgers traveled to San Francisco to face their arch rivals. The pennant race was tight; after winning two of the first three games of the series, the Dodgers led Milwaukee by just half a game and the Giants by a game and a half. On Sunday, August 22, they faced the Bull's old friend from the Dominican, Juan Marichal. Marichal was on his way to the first of many twenty-win seasons. He was facing Koufax in the concluding game of the series in a matchup of two future Hall of Famers. Marichal's baseball season was going splendidly, but just as John Roseboro and Maury Wills were dealing with larger conflicts off the field, so was Marichal. Throughout the 1965 baseball season the Dominican Republic had been in the throes of a civil war. The Dominican—where the Bull had played winter ball less than two years before and where Marichal had bailed him out of jail—had come apart in a coup. The Bull's driver, Mauesto, had perished in the conflict. Marichal's family was in the Dominican and in the middle of the fight. Complicating the entire situation was the position President Johnson had taken. Fearing another Cuba, he had ordered the intervention of American troops, and on April 30, 1965, the Third Brigade of the Eighty-Second Airborne Division landed in the Dominican. Ultimately more than twenty-thousand American troops were committed to the Dominican Republic as fighting continued throughout the summer on the streets of Santo Domingo. Marichal watched this all unfold on television, concerned for his family's safety. Willie Mays later said that Marichal was so distraught during this time that he should not have been playing baseball.

Those in the stands watching the game on August 22 saw a typically hard-edged Dodgers-Giants contest unfold. Maury Wills bunted his way on in the first inning and scored on a Ron Fairly double. Marichal apparently viewed the bunt as a cheap hit—since the end of the Dead Ball Era bunters have always faced this machismo prejudice—and brushed back Wills in his next plate appearance. Koufax retaliated in the bottom of the second by throwing a pitch over Willie Mays's head. A fierce competitor, Koufax did not believe in hitting opposing batters, but he did send messages. Firing back in the top of the third, Marichal brushed back Fairly, drawing a warning from umpire Shag Crawford. Now it was the bottom of the third, and Marichal was up to bat. Koufax's first and second pitches were not brushbacks; Koufax seemed to be putting the incident behind him. John Roseboro was not of this mind. Never one to back down from a fight—and he had just seen his community in flames two weeks earlier—Roseboro took action. His return throw to Koufax after the second pitch whizzed directly next to Marichal's ear. It may have even brushed it.

Buzzie Bavasi called John Roseboro "the Rock of Gibraltar." Although the reference was to the way he blocked the plate, it also denoted his toughness. He was so quiet in the clubhouse that he earned the ironic nickname of "Gabby," but he commanded the entire team's respect. He had just come from a week of defending his home in the tumult of the Watts riots. Marichal had experienced a civil war of another kind in his home country. Roseboro's throw nearly hit his ear, and Marichal turned toward the catcher. Roseboro started to come out of his crouch. He took off his mask. Some accounts say that words were exchanged. Umpire Shag Crawford claims that no words were spoken. Either way, Marichal raised his bat and hit Roseboro on the head. Twice. Blood streamed down Roseboro's face. Blinded by the blood, Roseboro lunged at Marichal. In a grainy YouTube video the action jumps from the pitch being delivered to the figures of Roseboro and Marichal halfway between the plate and the pitcher's mound. Marichal holds his bat high, and Koufax has raced from the mound and is trying to pull Roseboro away; Shag Crawford is pulling Marichal. Instantly players are surrounding the two. On-deck hitter Tito Fuentes advances with his bat raised. The Giants third base coach Charlie Fox runs in. Players flood in from the benches, and Willie Mays, number 24, is visible racing in from the dugout. Marichal is pulled to the ground, surrounded by players. Roseboro, his face covered in blood—Mays and Walter Alston thought his eye had been put out—furiously dives toward Marichal. The video ends there, and moments later Mays, a good friend of Roseboro's, leads him off the field. A furious Lou Johnson was restrained by the enormous Giant first baseman Willie McCovey. In the Dodger dugout Mays tended to Roseboro's head. Both fans and players could see this kind act, and it helped defuse the tension. Wes Parker felt that without Mays's presence there would have been a riot.

Marichal was thrown out of the game; Roseboro left to receive fourteen stitches. After fifteen minutes the game resumed, and the Giants went on to win, 4–3. It is amazing that Roseboro would only miss four games. His attorneys filed a lawsuit—although Roseboro was quoted as saying that Marichal's punishment should be ten minutes alone in a room with him. Marichal settled out of court for $7,000. Major League baseball suspended the pitcher for nine days and fined him $1,750, an amount that seemed even at the time to be a small price to pay given his action.

Years later Roseboro acknowledged that he had some culpability in the fight because of the throw that nearly nicked Marichal's ear. After Marichal initially lacked the votes to get into the Hall of Fame, Roseboro threw his support behind his old adversary, and Marichal went into the Hall of Fame in 1983. But that reconciliation was years away. In August 1965 the bitter Giant-Dodger rivalry could not have been more intense.

While the two Major League adversaries were engaged in another epic pennant battle, in Spokane, Washington, Al Ferrara was crushing the ball. He was on a roll, hitting as well as he ever had in his life. The team took a road trip to Hawaii. Because of the travel costs, Pacific Coast League teams would go to Hawaii once during each season and stay for seven or eight games. Ferrara explains: "You make only one trip because you don't wanna spend the money to keep going over there. We hardly ever won a game because everyone was partying." Earlier in July a reporter asked Al about the incident in Los Angeles that resulted in the

Bull's return to the Minors, and Ferrara nearly got into another fight. He stopped short of making his situation worse and continued his hitting streak. But he was exiled from glory. Like an actor giving a brilliant performance in a remote town far from critical acclaim, the Bull was living on the edge of oblivion. As August drew to a close and the Dodgers were in the thick of a four-team pennant race, Buzzie Bavasi was convinced the team needed another right-handed hitter. He dispatched Kenny Myers to Spokane to scout John Werhas. Myers arrived in Spokane in time to see the Bull scorch six doubles in three days. He called Buzzie and said, "You have your right-handed power hitter. It's Al Ferrara."

A moment of truth had arrived for Buzzie and the Bull. Buzzie's outrage over the drunk-driving incident was real. His vow that Ferrara would never play for the Dodgers again had been made in the heat of anger. But now there was a pennant on the line. Above all else Buzzie sought victory. If he looked for players with nerves of steel, he himself had to be expansive enough to accept those players with all their flaws if it meant winning one more game. On September 1 the Bull got the call: he was returning to the Los Angeles Dodgers.

September   **8**

The Bull joined the team on the road in Pittsburgh. The first day he arrived coach Preston Gomez, who would later manage the Bull for the Padres, took him aside and said, "Al, you gotta watch yourself. He's gonna be watching you." The Bull nodded and then that night went out drinking with his old friend Johnny Podres. For once they didn't get in trouble, but it illustrated the Bull's philosophy: "Put me on that field and I was gonna give you 100 percent, but I was also gonna give you 100 percent off the field." When Gene Mauch, the manager of the Philadelphia Phillies, was going over the Dodger hitters in a pregame meeting early in Ferrara's career, he got to the Bull and said, "I don't know too much about this guy. All I know is that he plays hard and he lives hard."

On September 1, the day Al got the official call back to the Major Leagues, the Dodgers dropped a doubleheader to the Pirates. Koufax pitched all eleven innings of the first game, losing, 3–2, and Drysdale lost the second, 2–1. The two best pitchers in baseball had taken the mound, but the result was two low-scoring, one-run losses. At the end of the day the Dodgers were in second place, one percentage point behind the Reds. Clustered closely behind were the Giants, Braves, and Pirates; four teams were within just 2 1/2 games of first place. Having joined the team in Pittsburgh, reunited with his old running buddy Podres, the Bull flew with the Dodgers to Houston, where they swept the Astros. Ferrara did not get on the field until the final game of the Astros series, when he made an appearance in left field late in the game. But he was back on a Major League diamond officially. The Dodgers returned to Los Angeles after a long road trip—a longer one for the Bull—and the Bull was finally, truly home again.

The Giants came to town and won a couple of close games, and then on September 9 an odd game was scheduled: the Chicago Cubs came to play a single game. At that time teams played a balanced schedule: teams in each league played each other a total of eighteen games, half at home and half away. This game was scheduled to fulfill that requirement. Sandy Koufax was the starter for the Dodgers and Bob Hendley for the Cubs. This game became the emblematic *mano-a-mano* of the era's pitching dominance. The Bull remembers the night vividly: "It was a beautiful night. You know how Dodger Stadium is in that third inning, where the lights start to set in and it's just getting dark and that background frames the stands." From the start the Bull could see that Koufax was on that night. His fastball was like an aspirin and "That [curve ball] was his big pitch of course; it differentiated him from everybody else—it looked like it disappeared. It would just fall off the table and disappear."

Vin Scully was in the announcers' booth for the Dodgers, and his call of the game has become part of his broadcasting legend. Scully was born in the Bronx in 1927 and grew up in Manhattan, a devoted Giants fan. After attending Fordham (where he played baseball, sang in a barbershop quartet, and did the radio broadcasts for various Fordham Rams sports), he spent two years in the navy and then got hired as a fill-in announcer for a CBS radio affiliate in Washington DC. After he impressed Red Barber by doing a play-by-play of a frigid football game atop Fenway Park—having forgotten his coat and gloves, thinking he would be in the press box—he joined Barber and Connie Desmond in the Brooklyn Dodgers broadcast booth in 1950. He was all of twenty-three years old and would spend the next sixty-seven baseball seasons announcing Dodger games. It is the longest run of any broadcaster with a single team. When the Dodgers moved to Los Angeles and were playing in the vast Coliseum, with its unfriendly sight lines, fans began bringing transistor radios to the game, knowing that Scully's play-by-play would guide them through the game. They continued the practice when the new Dodger Stadium opened, and throughout the ballpark one could hear Scully's calls. It was as if he were speaking to everyone in attendance and would occasionally act as an offstage prompter, suggesting a mass sing-along of "Happy Birthday" to an umpire. In his final week of broadcasting at Dodger Stadium Scully called the transistor radio "the greatest single break" of his career. In a farewell to his final game at Dodger Stadium, Scully said:

> Since 1958, you and I have really grown up together. Through the good times and the bad. The transistor radio is what bound us together. By the way, were you at the Coliseum when we sang happy birthday to an umpire? Were you among the crowd that groaned at one of my puns? Or, did you kindly laugh at one of my little jokes? Did I put you to sleep with the transistor radio tucked under your pillow? You know, you were simply always there for me.

By 1965 Scully was already perhaps the most popular man in Los Angeles, and on September 9 Sandy Koufax gave him one of the greatest baseball evenings ever to narrate in Scully's inimitable fashion.

The Dodgers and Cubs were two of the lowest-scoring teams in the National League, so it wasn't surprising that in the first couple of innings neither team got a runner to first base. Hendley was pitching well, and Koufax was his usual commanding self. Going into the fourth inning, there had still been no base runners for either side. As the top of the fourth inning ended, Scully noted, "We have a perfect game on both sides. Koufax has retired 12 in a row, Hendley has retired nine in a row and so there just hasn't been a visitor to first base." Hendley then pitched a one-two-three fourth inning, and Koufax continued the streak with a perfect top of the fifth. The Dodgers came to bat in the bottom of the fifth inning, and Scully set the stage: "No score. No hits.

Nothing but outs. Bob Hendley locked up in a perfect duel with Sandy Koufax."

Finally in the bottom of the fifth there was a base runner: Lou Johnson walked. He was sacrificed to second. With Hendley pitching to Jim Lefebvre, Johnson broke for third, attempting to steal the base. The catcher's throw sailed into left field, and Johnson raced home. The Dodgers were ahead, 1–0—and still without a hit. It was the epitome of the Dodger game—low-scoring, razor-edge, requiring nerves of steel. In the sixth inning Cub catcher Chris Krug hit a ground ball to Maury Wills. His throw was slightly off-line and hard to handle—but at first base was Wes Parker, a future Gold Glover. He handled it, and still no Cub had reached first base. Koufax struck out Hendley to end the top of the sixth, and Scully said, "Pass the word. For six innings, Koufax has pitched a perfect game. For five innings, Hendley has pitched a no-hitter."

The Dodgers went down in order in the sixth inning. Koufax struck out the first batter in the top of the seventh, got the second to fly out, and then fell behind Billy Williams, 3-0. Was he going to lose his perfect game? He got a called strike; 3-1. Williams fouled off a pitch. Full count. Then Williams hit the next pitch—a fly ball to Lou Johnson, who caught it. Going into the bottom of the seventh, Koufax still had his perfect game, and Hendley still had his no-hitter. Junior Gilliam grounded out to start the inning, and then Willie Davis was out on a superb fielding play by Ernie Banks, playing first base that day. Davis slid into first, but Banks applied a tag to get him out before he touched the base. Then Lou Johnson came up. He had been the only base runner in the entire game, and now he hit a little fly ball that fell into shallow right field. Johnson raced to second with a double, and the no-hitter was over. Walter Alston wanted his best defensive players on the field, and during the eighth inning John Kennedy warmed up in the tunnel so that he could replace Gilliam at third base. The man with whom he played catch was the Bull. Ron Fairly ended the inning by grounding out, and Koufax headed to the eighth inning, his perfect game intact.

Of the three major American sports—baseball, football, and basketball—only baseball has the possibility of perfection. The structure of football and basketball doesn't allow for perfection; teams can be shut out in football, and presumably they can be shut out in basketball (as happened occasionally in its primitive days), but there is no equivalent of the mathematical precision of lining up twenty-seven outs over nine innings. The only parallel occurs in another sport that is determined by someone controlling the path of a ball as it leaves the hand: bowling. The 300 game in bowling offers the same shimmering flawless form. But the difference is that the bowler is competing strictly against himself. Every other element is controlled. In baseball a pitcher faces a different batter three times an inning. His pitches are called balls and strikes by an umpire, who brings his own subjectivity to the game; one bad call and the perfect game becomes flawed by a walk. The tension of the perfect game builds toward its finality, and one can see this in the root of the Latin word *perficere*—to complete. Perfection is completeness. The moment something is not complete, it loses the possibility of perfection.

Sandy Koufax took the mound for the eighth inning. He was facing the cleanup hitter Ron Santo, followed by future Hall of Famer Ernie Banks and a rookie named Byron Browne. Walter Alston inserted John Kennedy to play third base; he was a better fielder than Gilliam. As Vin Scully noted, "John Kennedy is now at third base and I would think John Kennedy has as many butterflies as Sandy Koufax as you are put in the game as a defensive specialist and the pitcher has a seven inning perfect game—well, you know there is some pressure on you."

Koufax struck out Santo. Then he struck out Banks on a curve ball. Then he struck out Browne. The crowd rose to its feet, and Scully reported: "Sandy Koufax gets a standing ovation! He has struck out 11. He has retired 24 consecutive batters. In other words, he has pitched an eight inning perfect game. He's got three more outs to go." Scully always chose not to honor the baseball dugout tradition of not referring to the fact that a pitcher was throwing a no-hitter—he felt a duty to inform the fans of the game and not pussyfoot around the fact. By the time his lengthy career was over Scully would call twenty-one no-hitters, including a total of four by Koufax. And he had been behind the microphone on a national World Series broadcast for Don Larsen's perfect game in 1955.

Up until September 9, 1965, there had been just five perfect games thrown in the modern baseball era. It was the most unusual event in baseball. Coupled with what had been a double no-hitter for six innings, this game could go down in history as the best-pitched game of all time. And poor Bob Hendley who had retired the Dodgers in order in the bottom of the eighth and pitched the game of his life, would just be a historical footnote. Koufax took the mound for the top of the ninth. He was trying to finish his masterpiece, and Vin Scully would provide the most masterful commentary of his career.

Scully set the scene at the top of the inning: "Three times in his sensational career has Sandy Koufax walked out to the mound to pitch a fateful ninth where he turned in a no-hitter. But tonight, September the 9th, nineteen hundred and sixty-five, he made the toughest walk of his career, I'm sure, because through eight innings he has pitched a perfect game."

The first batter was Chris Krug. Koufax got ahead with two quick strikes. Scully: "You can almost taste the pressure now. Koufax lifted his cap, ran his fingers through his black hair, then pulled the cap back down, fussing at the bill." Koufax's next pitch was outside. Scully: "One and two the count to Chris Krug. It is 9:41 on September the 9th. The 1-2 pitch on the way: curveball, tapped foul off to the left of the plate. . . . There's 29,000 people in the ballpark and a million butterflies."

And now the Bull becomes memorialized in Scully's call: "Koufax into his windup and the 1-2 pitch: fastball, fouled back out of play. In the Dodger dugout Al Ferrara gets up and walks down near the runway, and it begins to get tough to be a teammate and sit in the dugout and have to watch." Hard to watch the ever-tightening tension of a perfect moment, but for the Bull, hard to watch any game from the bench. He was a baseball player, not a watcher; for players the point is always to be on the field. Peter Bavasi says, "I never watch a baseball game unless I'm being paid to do so." It's the motto of a professional. But the Bull, called back to the big leagues, was being paid to watch this game, and now he was pacing in the dugout, feeling the tension. Koufax's next pitch was outside for ball two. The crowd booed, and Scully said, "A lot of people in the ballpark now are starting to see the pitches with their hearts. The pitch was outside. Torborg tried to pull it over the plate but Vargo, an experienced umpire, wouldn't go for it. Two and two the count to Chris Krug. Sandy reading signs, into his windup, 2-2 pitch: fastball, got him swingin'!"

Koufax was now two outs away from a perfect game. The next batter was a pinch hitter, Joe Amalfitano. The on-deck hitter was Harvey Kuenn, pinch-hitting for the pitcher, Bob Hendley. Scully: "Kennedy is tight to the bag at third, the fastball, a strike. [It's] 0 and 1 with one out in the ninth inning. One to nothing, Dodgers. Sandy reading, into his windup and the strike 1 pitch: curveball, tapped foul, 0 and 2. And Amalfitano walks away and shakes himself a little bit, and swings the bat. And Koufax with a new ball takes a hitch at his belt and walks behind the mound."

The Bull often talks about the role of closers in modern baseball. Every great team now has a closer, the relief ace who comes in for the ninth inning and gets the save. The Bull maintains: "I played with the greatest closer of all time: Sandy Koufax. He got into the ninth inning of a game, and he got tougher and tougher. He was the best closer in baseball."

Now Koufax had two strikes on the second batter in the top of the ninth inning—two outs away from a perfect game. Scully:

I would think the mound at Dodger Stadium right now is the loneliest place in the world. Sandy fussing, looks in to get his sign, 0 and 2 to Amalfitano. The strike 2 pitch to Joe: fastball, swung on and missed, strike three! He is one out from the promised land, and Harvey Kuenn is coming up. . . . The time on the scoreboard is 9:44. The date, September the 9th, 1965, and Koufax working on veteran Harvey Kuenn. Sandy into his windup and the pitch, a fastball for a strike. He has struck out, by the way, five consecutive batters, and that's gone unnoticed.

The next pitch was very high; Koufax losing his hat on the pitch. He must have been feeling the extraordinary pressure of the moment. Scully noted that was only the second time all night that he felt that Koufax had thrown instead of pitched. Scully continues:

One and one to Harvey Kuenn. Now he's ready: fastball, high, ball 2. You can't blame a man for pushing just a little bit now. Sandy backs off, mops his forehead, runs his left index finger along his forehead, dries it off on his left pants leg. All the while Kuenn [is] just waiting. Now Sandy looks in. Into his windup and the 2–1 pitch to Kuenn: swung on and missed, strike two! It is 9:46 p.m. Two and two to Harvey Kuenn, one strike away. Sandy into his windup, here's the pitch: swung on and missed, a perfect game!

Then the radio audience heard thirty-eight seconds of cheering. Scully knew when to let the game play itself, to step back and allow the moment its drama without narration. Thirty-eight seconds later he spoke:

On the scoreboard in right field it is 9:46 p.m. in the City of the Angels, Los Angeles, California. And a crowd of 29,139 just sitting in to see the only pitcher in baseball history to hurl four no-hit, no-run games. He has done it four straight years, and now he caps it: on his fourth no-hitter he made it a perfect game. And Sandy Koufax, whose name will always remind you of strikeouts, did it with a flourish. He struck out the last six consecutive batters. So when he wrote his name in capital letters in the record books, that "K" stands out even more than the O-U-F-A-X.

There are a handful of elite athletes who confound sports fans' expectations. They are intensely competitive but lack showmanship. They are deeply intelligent but quiet. They have gravitas in sports that tend to celebrate boyish charm. In the 1960s basketball's Bill Russell, tennis's Billie Jean King, and baseball's Sandy Koufax were among these figures. All of them seemed to understand a larger dimension of life beyond sport: Russell fought for racial justice; King became a face for women's equality, and Sandy Koufax seemed to embrace the larger world of human spirituality beyond the baseball diamond. He was always aware of the fragility of the athlete. No one competed more fiercely, but his brushback pitches were never intended to hit and potentially injure a batter. They were messages, not malicious. In the press Koufax was portrayed as quiet and subdued. But the Bull remembers him in the clubhouse as one of the guys: fun-loving and always ready to joke around. "Koufax was magnificent," Al says. "The most dominating thing in the world. He was a mismatch against Major League hitters. But the greatest guy you'd want to have in a clubhouse." He could be insightfully funny. A reporter once asked Koufax how he pitched to Hank Aaron. He replied, "With nobody on."

One thing differentiated Koufax from other pitchers of the 1960s: after a start most pitchers took a day off—or two. They would go out drinking with their friends (consider Podres's and the Bull's many nights on the town) and would do so up until the day before their next start. Koufax began preparing for his next game the moment his previous start had ended. He was a consummate professional, previewing the modern era's demand for research and daily preparation. He was selfless in his pursuit of championships, literally sacrificing his arm for the Dodgers. Following a spring training game in 1965, Koufax awoke the next morning to find his left arm had hemorrhaged overnight. Dr. Robert Kerlan, the team physician, thought Koufax should restrict his pitching to once a week. Even at that, he might lose the use of his arm. Koufax chose to continue competing. He took pain medication every night and Butazolidin for inflammation. He applied "atomic balm" to his arm before every game and sometimes had to take additional pain medication in the fifth inning to make it through a game. In his final two years with the Dodgers Koufax would soak his arm in ice water for half an hour after each game, and it would still swell over an inch. His left arm became shaped like a parenthesis, and he had a tailor alter his suits to make the left arm an inch shorter. When he retired at the end of the following season, he explained that he was taking more pain medication and getting cortisone shots; the problem would only get worse with time: "I've got a lot of years to live after baseball and I would like to live them with complete use of my body." When Buzzie was asked how he planned to replace Koufax, he replied, "Here is a boy who has pitched four no-hitters, won twenty-seven games last season with arthritis, and is Jewish. Now, who can replace him?"

On that summer day in 1965 Koufax had achieved perfection; there was completion. Koufax hugged Lou Johnson; Cary Grant and Dyan Cannon sent catcher Jeff Torborg a congratulatory telegram, and for years Torborg would call Koufax on the anniversary of the perfect game. But in baseball ascending to a peak—unless it is the summit of winning the World Series—often means the only subsequent road is down. The season is too long to sustain pinnacles. A team cycles through hills and valleys, and before the cheapening effect of divisional or wild card play, it took six months to determine which team would win a pennant. Back before the perfect game on September 3 the San Francisco Giants had suddenly gotten hot and begun a fourteen-game winning streak. Dodgers fans could see that night after night the Giants' wins were piling up. On September 12 the Giants swept the Astros in a doubleheader and then beat them again the next day. They suddenly had a 2 1/2 game lead over the Dodgers with less than a month left in the season.

The Dodgers began their final road trip. In Chicago a rematch of Koufax and Hendley ended in a Cub victory. Meanwhile, the Giants scored three runs in the ninth inning to tie the Astros and then won the game in extra innings. It was now September 14, and the Giants' lead was 3 1/2 games.

The next day Don Drysdale was pitching in Wrigley Field.

Ernie Banks hit a line drive off his foot, and Drysdale had to leave the game. The Bull, for once, started the game in left field. He went 2 for 3 and drove in three runs. But as successful as the Bull was at the plate, it was as though the injury to Drysdale collapsed the Dodgers in the field. They made three errors and lost, 8–6. In Houston the Giants once again scored a run in the ninth to win a game. The Giants had won thirteen games in a row. At the end of the day the Dodgers were in third place, 4 1/2 games out of first.

On the morning of September 16, 1965, it rained in Chicago. It was cold, and only 550 fans had bought tickets to the game. This was before going to Wrigley Field became a social ritual beyond watching baseball for its own sake, before a JumboTron and walk-up music accompanied players to the plate, and before nonstop distractions—before the modern era, when teams feel a compulsion to distract ADHD fans who are essentially at odds with the natural pace of baseball. This was still a time when fans went purely to watch the game On a cold, wet day with the Cubs long out of the pennant race, a Chicago sportswriter noted, "There were more monkeys in Lincoln Park Zoo than there were cash customers on a grey and gloomy day."

Yet this day, the antithesis of days in sunny California, became a turning point in the season, and it pivoted when Walter Alston chose to turn to a man with nerves of steel. Claude Osteen had pitched well all season, even though he had woeful run support; in his first eight losses that year the team scored a total of thirteen runs. On this day he was pitching well. The Dodgers scored single runs in the first and second innings, and Osteen was taking a shutout into the ninth. But he walked the leadoff hitter, Billy Williams, bringing the tying run to the plate. Alston turned to his bullpen and made a startling choice. Coming in to try and win the game in relief: Sandy Koufax. Koufax had pitched six innings just two days earlier. He was going to face Ron Santo, Ernie Banks, and Harvey Kuenn. It was just the second time all year Koufax had pitched in relief. If the Dodgers lost this game—if their ace of aces failed in this most unusual situation, when it seemed

Alston was planting a flag as if to declare, "We make our stand here"—the season could well be over.

Koufax took the mound. Santo flied out to left. Banks popped out. Then Harvey Kuenn, who had been the final out of the perfect game a week earlier, lined out to second. The Dodgers won. The climb back up the mountain began.

Back in Los Angeles Buzzie Bavasi was like any other fan, listening on the radio. The deadline for trading was past. He could conceivably bring up additional players from the Minor Leagues, but there was no one left of value to bring up. The Bull was on the team, providing the right-handed power from the bench, and all Buzzie could do was watch as the drama of the final two weeks of the season unfolded.

The Giants finally lost a game when Hank Aaron hit two homers and the Braves crushed them. The same day, the Dodgers continued their road trip in St. Louis. Drysdale, recovered from the liner off his foot, or at least toughing it out, started against the Cardinals. Leading 3–0 in the sixth inning, he gave up a homer to Bill White and then a single. Walter Alston promptly brought in his closer, Ron Perranoski, to attempt a four-inning save. In today's game a two-inning save by a closer is a rarity, and the notion of a four-inning save is a baseball unicorn, reserved for the occasional World Series clinching game. But Perranoski did it. He allowed just one unearned run over four innings. The Dodgers won, and the Giants' lead was now 3 1/2 games.

On September 18 Sandy Koufax took the mound again. Two days earlier he had saved a game in relief. Now he was back as a starter. It had been a broiling hot day in St. Louis and had not cooled down much as the game began that night. Koufax pitched in this humid, steamy weather—and threw a shutout. A classic Dodger win, 1–0, on the strength of Koufax's complete game. But the Giants pitchers combined that day to throw a shutout of their own, so the Dodgers failed to gain any ground. The next day both teams won again. And the following day, Monday, September 20, when the Dodgers did not play, the Giants were again victorious. Now there were just twelve games left in the season. And the Dodgers were four games behind.

The Dodgers' road trip took them to Milwaukee. When the Dodgers were on the road, what did Buzzie Bavasi do to track their games? The same thing as every fan: he listened to Vin Scully and Jerry Doggett on the radio. He'd listen either on the car radio or on a transistor. Peter Bavasi remembers that Buzzie had various makes and models, "some of them serving as replacements for those that he broke after Vin or Jerry reported a Dodger miscue." If there was an injury or Vin reported an unusual happening, Buzzie would call the press box of the park in which the Dodgers were playing and speak with his traveling secretary, Lee Scott. Scully was adept at describing Walter Alston's game strategies, and Buzzie listened intently for those. If he had a question or disagreement about what Alston was doing, he'd wait until the club returned home before discussing it privately in Alston's clubhouse office.

During one road trip Buzzie's desire to listen to the game on the radio nearly got him into a misleading and embarrassing situation. He had traveled to Del Mar to take in a couple of days of horse racing with his friend Robert Kerlan. Evit, Buzzie, Kerlan, and his wife Rachel decided to have dinner in their rooms, so they got into their pajamas and robes and sat down to eat. The Dodgers had already won their day game, but Buzzie wanted to hear what the Giants were doing that night. He couldn't get the game on his transistor radio, so he proposed to Kerlan that they get in the car, go to the top of a hill, and see if they could pick it up on the car radio.

Kerlan agreed and drove them to a country lane atop a hill in La Jolla. They parked, still in their pajamas and robes. In *Off the Record* Buzzie wrote: "I had my head virtually in his lap to get my ear close enough to the radio in an attempt to find the game. Suddenly, I looked up and there stood the biggest cop you ever saw. He was shining his flashlight on us and asked, 'What are you doing?'

'You'll never believe this officer, but I'm trying to get a baseball game on the radio,' I said nervously.

'In your pajamas?'

I was envisioning the headlines in the paper the next day:
BAVASI, KERLAN IN SEX SCANDAL UP IN WOODS
Fortunately, the policeman let us go."

Buzzie would be listening to the radio as the Dodgers came to Milwaukee for a crucial series. The Braves were moving to Atlanta the next year; the two scheduled games were the final ones the Braves would ever play in Wisconsin. They had moved there from Boston just twelve years earlier, in the spring of 1953, the first modern-era baseball team to move west. Now they were headed south, a picture of mid-century American mobility. On September 21 Drysdale threw a complete-game win, and in Cincinnati the Reds scored six times in the sixth inning to beat the Giants. Eleven games left to play. The Dodgers were three behind.

One September 22 the Milwaukee Braves played their final game in County Stadium. Future baseball commissioner Bud Selig, who as a minority stakeholder in the team fought hard to keep the Braves in Milwaukee, noted that it was ironic the final game was against the Dodgers because Walter O'Malley had cited the successful move of the Braves in 1953 as support for moving the Dodgers west a few years later. Sandy Koufax started this game for the Dodgers, which was being televised in Los Angeles. It would provide Milwaukee with a startling contest to bid the Braves farewell.

The Bull started the game in right field and went 1 for 2, scoring a precious run. In the second inning Koufax gave up three singles, and then second baseman Frank Bolling came to bat. Although he had played in a couple of All-Star games, Bolling had never hit a grand slam in the Major Leagues. Koufax was off his game that day; he couldn't hit his spots. He fell behind, 3-0, and Bolling knew he had to throw him a strike. He did; 3-1. Then he threw another strike, and Bolling hit it over the wall in left field for a grand slam. In the third inning the Braves scored two more runs, and with the Dodgers trailing, 5–1, Howie Reed came on to relieve Koufax. Before he got out of the third inning, Gene Oliver hit an inside-the-park homer, and at the end of three innings the Dodgers trailed, 6–1.

It looked as though the game was a lost cause. But the Dodgers, in their characteristic fashion, never gave up. Jim Lefebvre hit a two-run homer. Then in the fifth inning both Willie Davis and Lefebvre hit RBI singles, and suddenly the game was tied. Earlier in this road trip, as noted, Ron Perranoski had delivered a four-inning save. Now Walter Alston called him in. He was asking him to attempt a five-inning save. Perranoski responded with a scoreless fifth, sixth, seventh, eighth, and ninth. But the Dodgers failed to score. The game went into extra innings. Perranoski pitched on—a scoreless tenth.

Finally, in the bottom of the eleventh inning, after Perranoski had thrown six shutout innings, Alston sent in a pinch hitter for his closer. Don Drysdale, an excellent hitter, batted for him and grounded out. Then Maury Wills came up. He singled. He would end the season with ninety-four stolen bases, but at this point Wills's legs were scarred, bruised, and exhausted. His team needed a run. He took off for second base—and slid in safely. Sweet Lou Johnson, playing in a pennant race for the first time in his long career, then hit a single, and Wills scored. The Dodgers had a lead. Bob Miller came on to pitch. Miller was a good friend of the Bull's, a fellow bon vivant. He wasn't normally the closer, but now he was being asked to end a crucial game. During a career in which he had played for ten different Major League teams, Miller was known as a utility pitcher; he could start, pitch in long relief, pitch in short relief—all as he overcame a perennial sore arm. His old teammate Roy Hartsfield (who later managed the Toronto Blue Jays for Peter Bavasi and Miller became their pitching coach) called Bob Miller "the Christian" because "he suffers so much. . . . When we came up with some other sore arms on the staff, he would come in and suffer a few innings." On this September evening Miller got one out, and then Mack Jones singled. Henry Aaron came up to the plate. How does one pitch to Hank Aaron? As Koufax had replied, "With nobody on base." Aaron hit a rocket to the outfield. Willie Davis raced in. Jones thought it was dropping for a hit and took off for second. Davis speared the ball and then threw back to Wes Parker at first base, doubling up Jones. The Dodgers won. And the Giants had lost. Ten games left to play. The Dodgers were now two games back, and they were returning to Los Angeles.

After the game fans wandered onto the field in Milwaukee, picking up souvenirs—such as home plate and the bases. The organist played "Auld Lang Syne," and a woman in a wheelchair approached Bud Selig. With tears in her eyes she implored him not to fail in his mission to bring baseball back to Milwaukee. He never forgot her plea, and five years later bought the bankrupt Seattle Pilots and returned Major League baseball to Wisconsin.

For fans at Dodger Stadium during the 1965 season, scoreboard watching was a dramatic event in itself. Rather than flashing information in blocks of text, the scoreboard scrolled out one letter at a time. Dodger PR director Red Patterson played with this unusual art form, ratcheting tension up letter by letter. On September 24 the Dodgers faced the Cardinals, while the Braves were playing the Giants. During the game the message board rolled out: M-E-A-N-W-H-I-L-E, I-N S-A-N F-R-A-N-C-I-S-C-O . . . B-R-A-V-E-S- . . . . Now Patterson would heighten the tension, adding more dots—. . . .—until finally posting "3." And then—G-I-A-N-T-S . . . more dots . . . 2. While this was unfolding, the Cardinals' Bob Gibson was shutting out the Dodgers. But in the seventh inning they pushed across two runs to take the lead. Two days earlier Ron Perranoski had thrown six innings in relief. Now he was called up to throw two innings and close the game. He did. Nine games left. The Giants' lead was just one game.

On Saturday, September 25, the Giants beat the Braves, 7–5. In Los Angeles Sandy Koufax started, following his uncharacteristic outing in Milwaukee. Now he returned to form. He shut out the defending world champion Cardinals, 2–0, and set a

new Major League record for strikeouts in a season. Bob Feller
held the old mark of 348; by the end of the season Koufax would
strike out 382.

The second half of the Dodger mighty duo, Drysdale, pitched
the following day. At this crucial juncture of the season, with
everything on the line, the Bull started in right field. He didn't
get a hit, but it was an indication that Walter Alston knew he
could count on him. The game's only run was manufactured by
Maury Wills: he hit a single; stole second, advanced to third on
an error, and scored on a fielder's choice. Drysdale pitched a
complete-game shutout. In San Francisco the Giants lost. That
score reached Dodger Stadium in time for the ninth inning. The
ballpark reverberated with a roar. The season had entered its last
seven days. Neither team would have a day off, and the Giants
and Dodgers had identical records.

On the first day of this final week the Giants beat the Cardinals in San Francisco. The Reds came to Dodger Stadium. With
the score 5–1 in the sixth inning, the bullpen gate opened, and
in came Ron Perranoski. He was asked to pitch the rest of the
game—four more innings. It was a bizarre move on several
fronts. With that large a lead, why turn to the closer? And why
ask him to pitch four innings? But pitch he did, letting in only
one unearned run, and the Dodgers won. In his last thirty innings
of pitching—littered with multi-inning stints—Perranoski had
allowed just two runs.

With both teams winning the night before, September 28 began
with the Dodgers and Giants tied for first place. The Cardinals
made short work of San Francisco, winning 9–1. In Dodger Stadium a Chavez Ravine pitching duel unfolded. The Bull started in
right field. He would go 2 for 3 in this game, and he also reached
base twice on walks. But the Dodgers couldn't drive him in. Claude
Osteen of the Dodgers and Jim O'Toole of the Reds pitched a scoreless game through six innings. Then the Dodgers scored a run
in the bottom of the seventh. The Reds countered with a run in
the top of the eighth. With one man out in the eighth and a tied
game, Alston called for a relief pitcher: Ron Perranoski, who had

pitched four innings the day before. Perranoski walked in and threw a scoreless ninth. The Dodgers couldn't score in the bottom of the ninth, and Perranoski took the mound for the tenth inning. Again no one scored. He pitched the eleventh, and again the Dodgers failed to score in their half of the inning. Finally, Perranoski was replaced by Howie Reed in the twelfth inning. Reed shut down the Reds. The stadium clock showed that it was almost midnight when Lou Johnson came to bat. Red reliever Joey Jay threw, and Johnson laced the ball into the left field pavilion for a walk-off homer. The Dodgers had done it. They were now in first place.

On September 29 the Giants played a day game in San Francisco, and the Dodgers played at night game in LA. Vin Scully and Jerry Doggett were on the radio in the afternoon, doing a recreation of the game at Candlestick Park. They got a pitch-by-pitch account and recreated the game as if they were there. It began as a rout, as Bob Gibson and the Cardinals led, 8–0, going into the ninth inning. Then the roof fell in. The Giants rallied, getting five men on board in the inning. Jim Davenport hit a three-run homer. They kept scoring. The Dodgers, warming up for their game, listened with increasing distress to the recreated play-by-play. When Willie Mays batted for a second time in the inning and singled to put the tying run on base, reliever Hal Woodeshick faced slugger Willie McCovey. A home run from McCovey would win the game. An astonishing comeback came down to this confrontation—and McCovey struck out. The Dodgers cheered in their clubhouse. Now they had to play their own game. They had Koufax going for them, the Reds had Jim Maloney, and the game was scoreless into the sixth inning. (How many games this season had unfolded like this?) Then the Dodgers loaded the bases, and Maury Wills drilled a triple down the right-field line. That was all Koufax needed. He got the win. Four games left. The Dodgers led the Giants by two.

The next day the Giants won—but Don Drysdale shut out the Braves, 4–0. The Dodgers had now won thirteen straight games. That streak had vaulted them past the Giants, and with

three games left to play the pennant was in sight. But all baseball streaks come to an end, and the next night the Braves'
Denny LeMaster shut them out. The Bull started in right field,
batting fifth. He didn't get any hits, but again he was in the
middle of the lineup in the most crucial week of the season. He
was back in the Majors and playing for a pennant. The Dodgers' streak was over that night, but the Giants lost to the Reds,
17–2. Two games left. Who would start them? Who else? Koufax and Drysdale.

The game on October 2 began as so many had that year: Koufax dominating an opponent and the Dodgers scoring a run without a hit. Junior Gilliam walked, stole second base, advanced to
third on a Braves error, and then scored on a wild pitch. It was
1–0, Dodgers, in nerves-of-steel fashion. The Braves tied it in
the fourth on a homer by Gene Oliver—the player who had beat
the Dodgers with a homer three years earlier to put them in a
playoff with the Giants. Certain players have a kind of voodoo
power over opposing teams, coming back to haunt them repeatedly. Would Gene Oliver once again tilt an entire season toward
calamity? In the bottom of the fifth the Dodgers loaded the bases
and then worked two walks off Braves pitchers. They were ahead,
3–1, scoring runs in their typical razor-thin manner of working
every angle. Koufax continued his dominating performance. At
the end of eight innings he had struck out twelve.

The Dodger Stadium scoreboard spelled out news of the Giants:
they had won their game. It was up to Koufax and the Dodgers.
If he could finish, the Dodgers had clinched the pennant. If not,
it was on to the final game of the season. The leadoff batter in
the ninth, Mike de la Hoz, singled. Then Koufax struck out Mack
Jones. De la Hoz tried to steal second as Jones struck out, and
John Roseboro threw him out. A strike-him-out, throw-him-out
double play. Then Koufax walked Woody Woodward. He started
pinch hitter Denis Menke out with a ball, and Walter Alston went
to the mound. Was Koufax done? Would Ron Perranoski make
yet another appearance? Koufax stayed in. As the Bull said, he
played with the best closer in the world—Sandy Koufax. Kou-

fax worked Menke to a 2-2 count. Then Menke lifted a fly ball to left field. Lou Johnson was there. Johnson caught the ball and rejoiced. He said after the game, "I squeezed that baby so hard and so long, there's nothing left of it."

The Dodgers had done it. They had climbed the mountain, and Buzzie Bavasi was overjoyed. He had started the season with a mission: to cement the Dodgers as a dynasty. He did it by assembling fearless players. Now they had one more series to win—the World Series. The Dodgers were off to Minneapolis to play the Minnesota Twins.

But Al "the Bull" Ferrara wouldn't be making the trip.

October   9

On a sunny afternoon in 2015 Al Ferrara stands outside the
entrance to the majestic Santa Anita Park racetrack, the San
Gabriel mountains framing it in the background. "This is my
Hawaii; this is my French Riviera. The characters, the bar, the
pageantry," he says. It has been four years since the Bull visited
Santa Anita in person—he wagers almost every day but does so
on his computer screen at home—but when he approaches the
will-call window, holding a bag with a sandwich from Clara's Italian Market, a gray-haired man steps out of the ticket booth and
extends his hand and greets him with, "Great to see you, Al. Let
me get you a box seat." If Ferrara has a band of brothers among
baseball players that binds and unites them all throughout time,
he has a second cohort within the world of horse racing. Everywhere he steps in Santa Anita, someone knows him—the ticket
taker, the bartender—and the two worlds even overlap as he
sees his old friend and fellow Dodger alumnus Bill Russell in
the track's clubhouse.

Al Ferrara grew up in a horse-racing culture. There was a
storefront on Twentieth Avenue in Brooklyn where two horse
handicappers—"the Commissioner," a large roly-poly guy, and
"Gene Shiny Pants"—had what amounted to an office. Everyone in the neighborhood bet on the horses; it was as much a
part of Brooklyn life as stickball and Junior's cheesecake. One
day the Commissioner came out to a baseball game in which Al
was playing at St. Anthanasius and told him, "I've got a horse

today that can't lose." After the game young Al walked in to the Twentieth Avenue storefront still wearing his baseball uniform. A clerk looked up from the card table where he was taking bets and saw Al, commenting, "Look at this. Who the hell is this? Whitey Ford?" He took Al's two-dollar bet. The horse came in seventh.

When it came to gambling, the Bull strictly kept himself to legal horse wagering. Or the greyhounds in Florida. The first sign a ballplayer sees in a clubhouse is "NO GAMBLING." The Bull adhered to that religiously. Baseball, after all, was his first love. While he might live on the edge, he would never endanger his future in baseball by betting on it.

Ferrara is clear about the chances of one's coming out a winner on a horse bet: "This is an opinion game. I spent a lot of my life before I realized I wasn't going to do this for a living. Talk about living on the edge. This is a game that can't be beat. Most days you come out here, you're gonna lose." He knows fully well that the science of racetrack wagering is at best risky, but he looks at it this way: "I'm going to blow my money somewhere. I might as well blow it here."

Santa Anita today stands as a glorious echo of another time, with its art deco Streamline Modern lines, painted in Persian green and chiffon yellow. Walking up green marble steps into the clubhouse, the Bull looks around at the deserted horseshoe-shaped bar. "Used to be nothing but people here," he recalls. "Lot of guys in the bar area standing around, trying to tout you. Now. . . ."

Al used to be a regular at Clocker's Corner, the dining spot at Santa Anita, placed where the horses race around the turn and head for home, sitting there with former baseball star Dick Allen and his old pal Jim Muhe. Muhe was the visiting clubhouse manager for the Dodgers from 1960 until 1990, a job that requires a tireless worker who handles the needs of a Major League team, from ordering uniforms (and the cleaning of uniforms); to ordering equipment (bats, pine tar, catcher's gear, gloves, shoes, etc.); to supervising bat boys; to sorting mail; to getting umpires four to five dozen game balls; to what might best be described as customer service (ordering postgame food spreads); to handling ticket requests. It's a Herculean job. For decades the Dodger clubhouse manager was Nobe Kawano, whose brother Yosh was the clubhouse manager for sixty-five years at Wrigley Field. The Kawanos might be the longest-serving brothers in Major League history. They grew up as baseball fanatics, hanging around Wrigley Field in Los Angeles (the Minor League park William Wrigley built). Yosh would sneak onto the ferry carrying the Cubs to their spring training site on Catalina Island, and at some point the Cubs let him start working for them officially. During World War II the brothers and their family were sent to an internment camp in Arizona; the Cubs secured Yosh's release so that he could work for the team. Clubhouse managers like Muhe and the Kawanos are part of the unseen architectural struts that support the action on the field. The topography of baseball is physical, sensual—horsehide, wood, neatly mown green grass, the leather of a glove—and all of it resonates with horses. Both worlds—baseball and horse racing—have deep American roots, reaching into the earliest days of the country. Horse racing was part of the national culture, a direct link to a time when everyone rode a horse. Now that the links to horsemanship have become archaic, the racetrack is no longer a social hub the way it was fifty years ago. But for baseball players there's always been an affinity to horse racing. During spring training going to the track at night was a natural activity for their competitive nature. And following retirement, as the Bull says, "There's those juices flowing, like when you were battling Seaver or Gibson. Your juices are flowing again—that's what we do for our competitive fix."

At Santa Anita Ferrara studies printouts he has brought from home, his personal racing form if you will. He ponders his options: "Something I really don't like about this [number] three horse . . . ; 7–2 isn't to my liking, so why try to buck it? . . . Like the 9–1. Never change the bet. . . . Horse comes out looking like he's come out of a car wash—sweating too much, too nervous. Seven in this race has early speed; he needs the lead. This jockey is a great gate rider. . . . This horse here—I'm gambling here—he's never run this length. . . . [For] the other horse, I'm using my handicapping skills. . . . If you don't like a horse—pass."

It has rained this morning, and that has radically altered Al's wagering strategy for the day. "I studied all night for a turf race," he explains. "Everything's all mumbled up. They've taken it off the turf, so now you're really gambling." He stands and watches the second race. He's bet on the number six horse, Maid Easy. They come out of the gate. Al tracks the race: "Six out there . . . good. . . . Stay up; don't let him come inside you." It's a seven-furlong race, and the horses make the turn and gallop down the straightaway to the finish line. The number eight horse—Comealongwithme—comes out of nowhere to win. The Bull shrugs: "That's life. There's always something that can screw you up."

In October 1965 the something that screwed up the Bull was the date of his return to the Major Leagues. September 1 started the cutoff period for the World Series roster. Those players on the roster the day before September 1 were eligible to play in the World Series. Those on the roster on September 1 or later were out of luck. The Bull was out of luck. He got the call up from Spokane on September 1, just hours too late to be on the World Series roster. He had played an integral role in the 1965 season—after all, the Dodgers had won the pennant by only two games. Ferrara had singlehandedly won the Ellsworth game, and the competitive edge he had brought to the field every day gave the Dodgers the lift they needed to fuel their spectacular September run. If an intangible can't be measured statistically, it can surely be proven at the finish line: the Dodgers won the pennant, and the Bull was one of the men that got them there. But now it was World Series time, and the door closed on the Bull. In today's game a team would have welcomed a non-roster player to accompany the team as a courtesy on the road trip to the World Series. But in 1965 as the Dodgers traveled to Metropolitan Stadium in Bloomington, Minnesota, Ferrara stayed in Los Angeles. The Dodgers were in the World Series. Ferrara was at the Mayfair, alone. Where could he go to assuage the pain of not being

with his teammates for the World Series? The horses were running at Hollywood Park.

Buzzie Bavasi was used to watching his teams play baseball in
October. Since he had taken charge of the team late in 1950, they
had played in six World Series; 1965 was to be their seventh. In
the first seventy-one years of their history the Brooklyn Dodgers won no world championships. Under Buzzie Bavasi they won
four in a span of eleven seasons. In the forty-nine years since he
left, they have won two. Bavasi always gave Branch Rickey credit
for building the great Dodger teams of the 1950s, but the truth
is that it was only under Bavasi that the Dodgers finally won a
World Series. Buzzie Bavasi had taken the team that Branch
Rickey built in the late 1940s, added Walter Alston as manager,
and led Brooklyn to its first—and only—world championship
in 1955. That team has been the subject of rhapsodies ever since,
from Roger Kahn's ode *The Boys of Summer* (a book that most
of its subjects hated because it presented them as mournful old
men instead of the happy and successful elders of the game they
were) to Doris Kearns Goodwin's *Wait Till Next Year*. Marianne
Moore's poem "Hometown Piece for Messrs. Alston and Reese"
ran on the front page of the *Herald-Tribune* on the first day of the
1956 World Series and confirmed that the Dodgers were worthy of
poetry. Indeed Bavasi was part of the second couplet of the poem:

> Buzzie Bavasi and the Press gave ground;
> the team slapped, mauled, and asked the Yankees' match,
> "How did you feel when Sandy Amoros made the catch?"

There was no poetry to celebrate the first game of the 1965
World Series. It was to be played, after all, at Metropolitan Sta-
dium, whose architectural style was famously described as "early
Erector Set." But the decision Sandy Koufax made about that first
game carried a poetic power: Wednesday, October 6, 1965, fell on
Yom Kippur, and Koufax declined to pitch. As his biographer Jane
Leavy remarked many years later, Koufax was not particularly
religious and his thinking was probably that the Dodgers had Don
Drysdale to pitch the opener, so it didn't make that much differ-

ence; Koufax would just pitch the next day. But the very fact that he acknowledged the importance of the holiest day of the Jewish calendar made his gesture perhaps more significant. If he had been a deeply observant Jew, there would have been no question of a choice, but Koufax made the choice to honor those of his faith and support them. It was a defining moment for a baseball superstar whose future had not always been assured. When the Dodgers signed him in 1954, he was an eighteen-year-old freshman at the University of Cincinnati. He was playing basketball for Cincinnati. Coming back to the East Coast in the summer, he tried out for the Giants at the Polo Grounds and then the Pirates at Forbes Field. Scout Al Campanis invited Koufax to an Ebbets Field tryout, with Walter Alston and Fresco Thompson looking on. Koufax started throwing. Campanis famously said later, "There are two times in my life the hair on my arms has stood up. The first time I saw the ceiling of the Sistine Chapel and the second time, I saw Sandy Koufax throw a fastball."

The Dodgers signed Koufax to a salary of $6,000 with a $14,000 bonus, which qualified Koufax as a "bonus baby," meaning that he had to stay on the Major League team for at least two years. The bonus baby rule was an anomaly of the time that certainly didn't help young players like Koufax develop. He pitched sporadically over his first three seasons, winning nine games and losing ten. In 1958 Koufax won eleven games, and the next year he struck out eighteen batters in one game. It was after the 1960 season that Koufax transformed himself into a superstar. He said, "I looked up and I had a few grey hairs—and I finally realized that either I was going to be really successful or I was in the wrong profession. Maybe the problem was that I never had a burning ambition to be a baseball player. If I had, I might have realized sooner just how much work was involved."

Koufax was blessed with "the left arm of God" but had never been passionate about playing baseball. The Bull was blessed with a burning passion to play baseball and made the most of the talent he had. Baseball is a game filled with the contradictory pulls of what God seemingly has given one man and what another man strives to achieve as a godly power. It is a game where the presence of the divine seems to hover over the field: had a foul ball hooked six inches fair and become a home run, Ferrara's 1965 season would have been radically different; if Tommy Davis had executed a different slide, his leg would not have been broken, altering the course of his career; if Sandy Koufax had not chosen to honor his religion's highest holy day, the world would not have had an example of respect that has influenced millions.

So it was that Don Drysdale started the first game of the 1965 World Series and the Bull went to Hollywood Park. Before the series began, Buzzie predicted the Dodgers would win it in four games, setting off a small firestorm in Minnesota. To placate the Twins he showed up in Minneapolis wearing a "Go Go Twins" button. His confidence—or salesmanship—was perfectly logical. As he said to Sid Ziff of the *Los Angeles Times*, "I don't think the competition from the Twins will be any tougher than the Yankees when we beat 'em four straight." He lived to regret his prediction. In the third inning of Game One the Twins batted around, scoring six runs off Drysdale. When Alston walked out to the pitcher's mound to put in a reliever, Drysdale said, "I bet right now you wish I was Jewish, too." The Twins ended up winning the game, 8–2, behind the pitching of Jim "Mudcat" Grant. Grant felt he didn't really pitch well; his curveball wasn't effective. Before one of his at bats Grant shared this information with Vice-President Hubert Humphrey, sitting in a box seat. Humphrey suggested he stick with his fastball.

Although seeing Drysdale lose like that was not how Buzzie Bavasi imagined that the series would begin, now he had Sandy Koufax pitching in Game Two. The day of the game was drizzly and cool. Koufax and Twins pitcher Jim Kaat, who had won eighteen games that season, were both pitching shutout baseball through the first five and a half innings. Kaat had been helped by a spectacular diving catch by his left fielder, Bob Allison, in the top of the fifth that stymied a potential rally. In the bottom of the sixth Zoilo Versalles led off with a ground ball to third. It bounced off Junior Gilliam's glove, and Versalles ended up on second base. He scored on Tony Oliva's double, and then Oliva scored on Harmon Killebrew's single, and the Twins had a 2–0 lead off the world's best pitcher. The Dodgers rallied in the seventh, scoring a run and getting men on second and third with just one out. Koufax was due to hit, but Walter Alston decided to pinch hit for him. He sent up Don Drysdale, a move that might seem unusual, except that Drysdale actually held the best batting average on the team. He hit .300 in 1965 and also had seven homers in just 130 at bats. It was a situation that called for a right-handed power hitter—someone like the Bull. But Don Drysdale was the best option the Dodgers had. Before the World Series began, Buzzie Bavasi had been asked if he had thought about trading for a power hitter. "Of course I did," he replied. "But we couldn't get anyone we wanted." He referred to Frank Thomas (a different Frank Thomas from the Chicago White Sox power hitter) whom the Milwaukee Braves acquired. Bavasi continued, "Thomas was offered to us. With all due respect to him—he's a nice guy—he just didn't fit into our plans. So the Braves took him. Where did they finish?" The answer, of course, was that they finished far out of contention. So with the Bull back in Los Angeles watching on television, Don Drysdale came up with a chance to put the Dodgers ahead in the game and pull even in the series. He struck out. Maury Wills made the third out, and the Dodger threat was over. The Twins went on to add two more runs when, ironically, their pitcher, Jim Kaat, drove in a couple with a single, and they won the game, 5–1. The Dodgers, who had been favored to win the series, headed back to Los Angeles down 2–0. On the plane back player after player came up to Claude Osteen, who would start Game Three, assuring him that "he'd get them." Osteen said later, "By the time I got off the plane, I was a nervous wreck."

Osteen, as noted, had been the pivotal man in the Frank Howard trade. He showed up for spring training at Vero Beach, and Dick Tracewski quickly nicknamed him "Gomer" for his resemblance to the actor Jim Nabors, who played Gomer Pyle on television. Like Gomer, Osteen was indeed a country kid to start out with, growing up in the small town of Caney Spring, Tennessee. He perfected a curve ball at an early age, and it made his rural team, the Woodman Choppers, a baseball powerhouse. By the time Osteen was in high school, his family had moved to a suburb of Cincinnati, where Osteen posted a 16-0 record, with a 0.13 ERA, as his team won the state championship. He matured as a pitcher in his time with the Washington Senators, and he came to the Dodgers as a savvy pitcher who had developed terrific command, learned how to change speeds, and could identify a hitter's weakness. Osteen, moreover, immediately noticed the Dodger culture: "Dodgertown was a big family." This has become a cliche of sports—the concept of creating a family within a business proposition—but the feeling at the Dodgers was genuine. At the end of the 1965 season pitcher Roger Craig (who had formerly been with the Dodgers but in 1965 pitched for Cincinnati) was asked by the *Los Angeles Times'* Sid Ziff how the "timid-hitting Dodgers are leading the National League." Craig responded, "It is a happy ball club, and that happiness stems from the top; right from Buzzie Bavasi on down to the bat and ball boys. Where lots of clubs go out of their way to make one or two stars happy, the Dodgers take care of the players right down the line and you gotta pinpoint Bavasi for being responsible." He gave an example of what he was talking about. Following spring training in 1959, he was sold to Spokane and had to take a $1,500 pay cut. Craig went to Bavasi to ask him to stipulate in his contract that he'd get the money back if he returned to the Major Leagues. Craig says, "Buzzie said he didn't like the idea but promised if I made it, he'd take care of it. The Dodgers bought my contract back in June and my first start was against Cincinnati." Bavasi met him in the tunnel right after the game, shook his hand, and congratulated him. "Imagine my surprise when I took my mitt away and found a fifty-dollar bill in it." He said that Bavasi told him, "Go take your wife out and have a good time." The next day he called Craig in and asked how he wanted the $1,500—in a lump sum or spread out over the year. Craig concludes, "You gotta play your heart out for a guy like that and I wound up with my best year."

Now the Dodgers fate was in Gomer's hands. If they lost this game at home, they would be in the impossibly deep hole of trailing three games to none. Osteen faced the first batter of the game, Zoilo Versalles, and he promptly hit a ground-rule double. He advanced to third on a ground out. Given the Dodgers inability to score runs, this situation represented an immediate existential threat to their season. Tony Oliva grounded out, and Versalles stayed at third. Two down. Harmon Killebrew, the Twins big slugger, walked. Catcher Earl Battey came to the plate, and third base coach Billy Martin flashed a hit-and-run sign. Battey missed the sign. He took the next pitch; Killebrew took off for second base but then stopped. John Roseboro's throw down to second was alertly caught by Maury Wills (who was always alert); Wills saw that Versalles had taken off for home. He threw home, and Versalles was out in a rundown. Disaster had been averted.

Osteen went on to pitch a complete-game shutout, the kind of dominating pitching performance the Dodgers had anticipated from Koufax and Drysdale. The Dodgers won, 4–0, and it was as if the team reset itself. The next day was a rematch of the Game One pitchers, and this time Drysdale and the Dodgers dominated. They won going away, 7–2, and the series was tied. Next pitcher up for the Dodgers: Sandy Koufax. Now it was Koufax's turn to pitch true to form. He shut out the Twins, 7–0, striking out ten. The Bull watched these games as a spectator at Dodger Stadium, in the strange netherworld of being part of a team but not being on the team. The Dodgers flew off to Minnesota for the final game or games of the season; the Bull stayed behind.

The Twins had played poorly in Los Angeles, making fielding errors and base-running miscues. Now they were home, and Twins manager Sam Mele turned to his ace, Mudcat Grant. Grant had had just two days of rest. He woke up the morning of the game with a cold. He told a reporter, "My head feels like a balloon, my cold's no better and my knees are bothering me. Otherwise, I'm all right." Claude Osteen was pitching for the Dodgers, and both pitchers started well. The game was scoreless until the fourth inning, when Bob Allison hit a two-run homer for the Twins. That was all Mudcat needed. He pitched superbly the rest of the day—and even belted a three-run homer to deep left-center. The Twins won the game, 5–1. Now the 1965 season was coming down to the final day, the final game. And Sandy Koufax would take the mound.

Back in Los Angeles the Bull pondered where he should go to see the game. Where would he feel at home and in a company of people that knew instinctively the ups and downs of life, a group that understood that in life, there's always "something that can screw you up"? Al states: "I went to the Hollywood track and did a run on the trotters, and of course they had TVs on, and I watched the game." It was there at the Hollywood Park bar, in between tracking his bets on the trotters, that Ferrara watched Sandy Koufax take the mound for Game Seven.

Koufax was starting his third game in eight days. All season long he had battled traumatic arthritis in his left elbow with cortisone shots, codeine, Butazolidin (a drug prescribed for horses), and Capsolin, a pitcher's salve that was manufactured from hot chili peppers. When he shook hands with Twins starter Jim Kaat, Kaat's eyes burned from the exposure to all the ointments. By Game Seven Koufax was literally pitching on fumes. In the bottom of the first inning Koufax walked two batters, and Don Drysdale got up in the bullpen. Catcher John Roseboro repeatedly called for Koufax to deliver a curve ball, and Koufax shook him off. Roseboro ran out to the mound, and Koufax told him his arm wasn't right. It was sore. Roseboro said later that he asked Koufax what they should do, and Koufax replied, "Screw it; we'll blow 'em away." So he did. He threw inning after inning with just one pitch—his fastball. He mowed through the Twins, dodging a bullet in the third inning when Zoilo Versailles stole second but was called out for interference. Sweet Lou Johnson told Koufax before the fourth inning that he would get him a run—the only one he would need. And he did. He hit a home run off the left-field foul pole. Dodgers 1, Twins 0. Ron Fairly followed Johnson's homer with a double, and then Wes Parker drove him in. The Dodgers had a 2–0 lead, and Superman was on the mound—throwing just one pitch. Koufax went into the ninth inning clinging to the 2–0 lead.

The ninth inning would be the 360th inning he had pitched that season. The middle of the Twins order was up. The first batter, Tony Oliva, grounded out. Then Harmon Killebrew singled. Now the tying run came to the plate, Earl Battey. Koufax struck him out. Bob Allison came up, the Bob Allison who had hit a bases-loaded double off Koufax earlier in the series. Koufax bore down one more time—and struck out Allison. The Dodgers were world champions. Koufax was too tired to even raise his arms in celebration. His season was over. He had struck out 411 batters, going 28-9, with a 1.93 ERA.

Back in Los Angeles the Bull was at Hollywood Park, betting on the trotters. As the game drew to a close, he sat at the bar, rooting intensely. There was a championship at stake, but there was also money on the line for Ferrara. After the World Series, players get shares of postseason revenue based on gate receipts. Those shares are determined at a players-only meeting held near the end of the season. Full-time active players get a share as a matter of right, but because of the timing of his return to the club, Ferrara was not a full-time player. What, if anything, he would receive was up to his teammates. In a testimony to the value his fellow players saw in him, at that meeting they voted the Bull a full share. Ferrara couldn't know the value of his share until after the World Series—the champions got more than the losers. All he knew was that his teammates thought enough of him to give him a full share. And he knew that his salary was $11,000 a year. If the Dodgers won, it was possible that his share of the championship purse would be close to that much again.

Ferrara remembers, "I went to that bar and I watched that TV, that last pitch, because it was gonna be the difference of whether I stayed in the penthouse or an outhouse." Koufax didn't let him down, Ferrara adds: "He was just the most dominating thing in the world; he was fantastic. He was such a nice guy, not only a great pitcher, but a great guy." For people wagering on horse races there is no other focus than their pick and their race. Ferrara was alone on his perch at the Hollywood Park bar stool as he cheered Koufax's final strike. He raised his arms in celebration. He cheered the TV set: "Way to go, Sandy!" His team had won. He was a world champion. He was part of one of the great dynasties in American sports history. Then he gathered himself off the bar stool and went to place his bet on the next race.

Fifty years later, in his Studio City apartment, the Bull sweeps his hands open wide. He always gestures with his hands; it's the lineage of his mother, the passionate one in the family, the glue that held things together. Al explains: "That '65 season was very tumultuous for me. I mean the range of emotions that I had— getting sent down, coming back, the Ellsworth home run, the world championship. . . . Being embarrassed about the way I acted. . . . But that was it. No excuses. I always said in my life, 'If you're gonna do something, be able to pay the consequences, take responsibility for those actions.'"

The long season was over. There was a big party at Dodger Stadium in the Stadium Club. They were all there, the team in all its expansive forms: Buzzie Bavasi had a cigar with Walter O'Malley. Fresco Thompson was laughing with Walter Alston. Maury Wills, the spark plug, could finally relax and look forward to the offseason and the chance to heal his legs. Koufax and Drysdale, the mighty pitching duo, so fierce on the mound, were now joking with their teammates. John Roseboro and Junior Gilliam, Ron Fairly and Sweet Lou Johnson—the guys with the nerves of steel were all gathered together. Jim Muhe was drinking with Nobe Kawano. Al "the Bull" Ferrara walked in. He saw Johnny Podres, and they hugged. They had lived through the summer of 1965— the promise of spring training; the disappointments of sitting on the bench; the sudden victory that came with a home run; the craziness of a world turned upside down as quickly as a car turns up an exit ramp; the burning rage of a dream deferred that set Los Angeles afire; the perfection of Sandy Koufax; the thrill of a pennant race that seemed lost and then turned within three weeks to a startling victory. It had been a year for the ages, for the Dodgers, for Los Angeles, and for Ferrara. He looked across the room, and there was Buzzie Bavasi. The Bull walked over to Buzzie and the two men embraced. "Hell of a year."

The next day the party was on at the Mayfair, as Al comments: "The same stuff; the town was partying; they were all coming down to the Mayfair to say hello." When the party finally died out, Ferrara was alone. His running buddy Johnny Podres had gotten married and now spent the winter back in his hometown in upstate New York.

The Bull had been a crucial part of a world championship team. Today virtually everyone associated with a World Series winner gets a ring—the equipment manager, the clubhouse guys, players who barely played on the squad. The top of the 1965 World Series championship ring is a circle of brilliant blue with a diamond set in the center. It is a diamond in the baseball sense, a baseball diamond, with a clear diamond gem filling the base paths. Circled around the blue are the words "Los Angeles—World Champions." One side of the ring is emblazoned with the Dodger logo. The script of "Dodgers" sits above the interlaced LA; a baseball soars above the logo, as if it is one of the rarely hit homers from that year. The other side of the ring features a baseball in front of two crossed bats. A player's individual name is written across the baseball. In 1965 the only players who received world championship rings were those on the roster for the actual series. The Bull explains this in his apartment, with his hands spread wide. He does not have that ring.

Winter   **10**

When Al Ferrara was playing for the Atlanta Crackers in 1961, he met a young woman named Norma Jean, a truly beautiful southern belle. After the 1965 World Series Norma Jean called up the Bull and said she was coming to Los Angeles to visit him. It was an awkward moment; it had been a few years since they had seen each other, but that was not the real issue. Ferrara was still living at the Mayfair Hotel, but a problem had arisen. Typically enough, it concerned the payment of his bill. The Mayfair management contacted Buzzie Bavasi—apparently anything to do with the Dodgers or their players went through Buzzie—and let him know that the Bull owed the Mayfair $4,800. Buzzie called Ferrara into his office and asked him how much his rent was at the hotel.

"Two dollars a day."

"How can you owe them $4,800?"

"Well," the Bull explained, "you know . . . this and that. I'd go to the track and say, 'Gimme a hundred dollars and put it on my bill at the Mayfair.' And there's a lot of people that work at this hotel—waiters, waitresses and the like. All the wonderful bartenders there at the hotel need to be taken care of. If I didn't spend this type of money on a regular basis, these people would be out of work; they would have no place to go, so I feel like that I'm contributing to society by doing things like this."

"Well, I have news for you. You've done a terrible job of taking care of the Mayfair," said Buzzie. "It's going bankrupt. The good news is you only have to pay 10 percent of what you owe, but you've gotta get out of there."

The timing was unfortunate, as Norma Jean was arriving in Los Angeles, expecting the Bull to wine and dine her. He had to take her somewhere, though the truth was that at the moment he was a man without a home. The Bull sadly bid farewell to the Mayfair: "I'm out of the Mayfair. I had this place, perfect, in an area where I could walk to. I had all of the strip joints, the go-go bars; they were all in that area. I lost my Casbah." Ferrara considered his options. He was temporarily homeless and low on funds as usual, so he made a typically rational choice: he checked into the famed Ambassador Hotel. He took Norma Jean to the Coconut Grove for three nights of cocktails and high living, and when she finally left for the airport, the Bull's first thought was, "I gotta go to Buzzie and get money to pay for this damn bill." He explained to Buzzie that he was in between residences and that when Norma Jean showed up, he had to check in somewhere. Buzzie marveled at this latest display of Ferraranomics, but this was simply the beginning of the Bull's new budgeting technique: "I wound up being the King of Plastic." Ferrara's financial rescue in the mid-1960s came in the form of the credit card explosion that seized America. It was incredibly easy to get a credit card, and the Bull had "every credit card in the world. . . . I was loaded for bear."

Al found a place to live that was another excellent match: the Blair House. It was a long-term residence apartment building in the middle of Hollywood, near Melrose and Vine. The owner was eager to build a clientele of celebrities, and at that moment in Los Angeles the Dodgers were enormous stars. The owner offered Ferrara a discounted room in return for his bringing players to stay at the Blair House during the season. The Bull was happy to oblige, and he eventually occupied the penthouse free of charge. The Blair House became another gathering point for mayhem and marked his entrance into the world of Hollywood.

While Ferrara was settling into his new residence, Buzzie Bavasi was dealing with another strange new world. In January 1966 young Bill Bavasi was riding in the back seat of his parent's car. His ears pricked up, as they always did, when he heard his father mention his favorite Dodger players. This time he overheard Buzzie say to Evit, "There's going to be trouble with Sandy and Don." He didn't realize what that meant at the time, but soon the entire world knew: baseball's two best pitchers were holding out for a more equitable wage. There had been holdouts in baseball before, but this was the first time that two of the game's biggest stars had joined forces in a salary negotiation. They asked for a three-year, million-dollar deal. It would be split equally so that each would earn $167,000 per year. The two stars were tired of being played off each other when it came time to negotiate salaries; they'd hear, "I'll pay you next year, Don, but this year we have to pay Sandy." At the time Willie Mays was baseball's highest paid player, with a salary of $125,000 a year. In his historic 1965 season Koufax earned $85,000, and Drysdale was paid $80,000. Buzzie Bavasi's offer for 1966 was $100,000 to Koufax and $85,000 to Drysdale. Koufax and Drysdale responded with their mini-union, asking that Bavasi negotiate with their agent, J. Alfred Hayes—and the battle was on. (Walter O'Malley had warned his "boys": "As you go through life, don't trust anybody who uses an initial for his first name.") This was a full two years before the players' union executive director, Marvin Miller, negotiated the first collective bargaining agreement. Koufax and Drysdale were on their own, staking out new ground.

The stance of the two dominant pitchers of their time set off shock waves, in part because Koufax requested that he be represented in the negotiation by an agent. He said, with complete justification, that every American had the right to representation. That's not how Major League baseball saw it, however. Buzzie replied that he would talk with an agent but insisted that the actual negotiation be conducted directly with Koufax. On one level his agenda was clear: Bavasi was a professional negotiator and dealing directly with the players gave him an enormous advantage. But he had a vision of the deluge to come, which he articulated in a *Sports Illustrated* article the following year: "If I gave in and began negotiating baseball contracts through an agent, then I set a precedent that's going to bring awful pain to general managers for years to come, because every salary negotiation with every humpty-dumpty fourth-string catcher is going to run into months of dickering."

That dickering has now evolved into a full-time job, just as Bavasi predicted. Bavasi may have seen catastrophe on the horizon, but he continued to have fun. At the start of the holdout, as a joke, he posed kneeling in prayer before photos of Koufax and Drysdale.

Koufax and Drysdale didn't report to spring training and instead stayed in Los Angeles, determined to get better contracts. They had two sources of leverage. One was public: in March both signed contracts with Paramount Pictures to appear in the movie *Warning Shot*, starring David Janssen. They were scheduled to work for two weeks, portraying a TV commentator and a police sergeant, and they appeared at Paramount with Janssen for a PR shoot. It was a mob scene, with dozens of reporters and TV cameras focused not on the film but on the holdouts. The other source of leverage was an internal conviction Koufax held that he would play for only one more season. If the Dodgers didn't make a deal, he was comfortable retiring before his arm was permanently damaged. Koufax and Drysdale were operating on their own, without agents, but it was an early sign of the seismic shift in the world of baseball. The players were beginning to exert their power.

For Buzzie it was a confounding situation. He was tasked by his owner with maximizing profit. Walter O'Malley certainly was nothing if not concerned with making money, and yet he consistently reinvested in his team. Buzzie knew how vitally important Koufax and Drysdale were to the Dodgers' success. There had probably never been as devastating a one-two pitching punch in the history of the game. And both were exemplary characters. According to his memoir *Off the Record*, Buzzie had allocated about $100,000 for Koufax and $90,000 for Drysdale. If one is to believe Buzzie's narrative, he was convinced that the two could be signed easily, but "The hold-outs were making headlines in every paper in the Los Angeles area every day." Bavasi thought that eight weeks of spring training wasn't really necessary, especially for Koufax; two weeks were plenty of time to get ready. He explained to Walter O'Malley, "We can settle this in five minutes, but we'd lose all those headlines." Bavasi claims that O'Malley played along, leaving phone messages for Koufax and Drysdale when he knew they'd be out; then when they returned his calls, he would tell reporters that they were "anxious to come back, that they were calling every day."

In the end Bavasi credits former Dodger and star of TV's *Rifleman* series, Chuck Connors, with being the diplomatic go-between. Connors was close to all three parties and arranged a meeting in Los Angeles. They agreed on a salary raise that was intended to give them equal amounts but ultimately came down to $125,000 for Koufax and $110,000 for Drysdale—thus a raise of $40,000 for Koufax and $30,000 for Drysdale. A key to understanding what happened here, and to the world that Bavasi had to navigate in the 1960s, is that Bavasi never had the luxury of setting a budget for the team salaries. Buzzie would annually make his best case to Walter O'Malley, who set the budget, delineating the amount within which Bavasi had to maneuver. For the 1966 season O'Malley had prescribed $100,000 in salary increases for the entire team. Bavasi was now in the position of giving $70,000 of that to Koufax and Drysdale; the rest of the team had to split just $30,000 in increases. In order to make this negotiation reasonably pencil out for the whole team, Buzzie had to go back to O'Malley for more based on these highly unforeseen circumstances. O'Malley agreed to most of what Buzzie was after, but Buzzie still needed a touch more to make it work, and he ultimately signed the deal for that added amount. While O'Malley took a haircut, Buzzie ended up taking a shave himself. That Christmas O'Malley sent Bavasi a holiday card that included a check and a note. Buzzie saw that the check was a bit lighter than previous annual bonuses, but he had to chuckle and agree with O'Malley's handwritten note, which said, "Merry Christmas, Buzz. How good of you to give part of your Christmas bonus to Sandy and Don."

Bavasi had to rely on all his negotiating skills—and wiles—to bring the rest of the team's salaries in line that year. It was an enormously difficult juggling act and a precursor of the upcoming joyless world of negotiating with agents. Koufax and Drysdale were pioneers; they were exerting their lawful rights, but the end result was baseball had been pointed in the direction of a corporate rather than a personal (and yes, paternal) relationship between players and management.

A year later Bavasi noted, with characteristic hyperbole: "When the smoke had cleared, [Koufax and Drysdale] stood together on the battlefield with $235,000 between them, and I stood there with a blood-stained cashbox." And he added: "Be sure to stick around for the fun the next time somebody tries that gimmick. I don't care if the whole infield comes in as a package; the next year the whole infield will be wondering what it is doing playing for the Nankai Hawks." Buzzie had seen the future, and he knew it. Soon enough, the players' union would indeed come in as a package of all Major League baseball players. But there have been few blood-stained cash boxes; baseball has thrived both on and off the field ever since the advent of free agency.

Buzzie's comment about the "blood-stained cash box" was part of an unprecedented four-part series in *Sports Illustrated* that appeared in the winter of 1967. It was a remarkable series in part because of its sheer volume: four articles in four consecutive weeks, all about Bavasi and the Dodgers. It speaks to the prominence of the team in the 1960s; under Buzzie's leadership they had indeed supplanted the Yankees as baseball's dominant champions. The series was in the form of as-told-to pieces under the general title "The Dodger Story," by Buzzie Bavasi with Jack Olsen. Part 1 was Buzzie's account of "The Great Holdout," which started with the bit about the blood-stained cashbox. It detailed his side of the negotiation, salted with praise for Sandy Koufax as upright, scrupulously honest, and an impeccable competitor. He vowed that the strategy of a double holdout would never work again: "The plan only worked because the greatest pitcher in baseball was in on it, and also they caught us by surprise." And he referenced the fact that because he paid Koufax and Drysdale more than anticipated, he couldn't give raises to other players. Part 2, "Money Makes the Player," may have been the piece in the series that had, as Peter Bavasi notes, the most unintended of unintended consequences in helping to rally a players' union. Buzzie describes his joy in negotiations:

> Just on the face of it, you'd think I'd be miserable, arguing and cajoling and disagreeing with the guys I like the best in the world, but I like to argue and cajole and disagree, and so do most of my ballplayers. They bring their competitive spirit right up to my office. . . . Anything goes at salary time. . . . I honestly don't think I'd hold it against a ballplayer if he pulled a knife on me and ordered me to sign him up at a higher figure. He knows I'd pull my own knife the next year, and we'd both wind up laughing about it later. We always do.

Buzzie was right when he described his players as "the guys I like the best in the world"; it was the players, after all, who bought Bavasi a boat with their own money when he left the Dodgers. Reggie Jackson (who played for Bavasi years later as an Angel) described Buzzie as an avuncular uncle: "To me, Buzzie is the kind of guy who was born at the age of 60 and will always be 60. He is always your dad, always your father. . . . I feel I could phone Buzzie any time, for any kind of advice. Or I could stop in and have lunch or dinner with him. I feel I could phone him to borrow twenty-five hundred dollars any time. That's the way Uncle Buzzie is."

Chuck Connors makes an appearance in the article beyond acting as a mediator during the Koufax-Drysdale holdout: Bavasi says that he would mail him a contract signed in blood. It was actually red ink, but Connors would come to Bavasi's office and swear he'd opened a vein and signed the contract because "you might as well have my blood; you've got everything else."

It was in this section of the four-part series that Bavasi tells the story of the dummied-up contract. He had his secretary, Edna Ward, fix a phony contract calling for $9,000 for Tommy Davis after he'd won the National League batting championship. He'd leave the Davis "contract" on his desk and then excuse himself mid-negotiation with a young player. The player wouldn't be able to resist looking at the contract. When Buzzie returned, he said, "Have you thought any more about it?" And the player said, "Maybe I'm being unreasonable." He'd offer to sign for $12,000; Buzzie would give him $18,000. Buzzie's technique may have been Machiavellian, but his intended result was for the player to feel good about his deal. Buzzie figured it gave his team a competitive advantage if he could get all the players feeling happy going into the season. Whatever his intention, Bavasi's revelations of how management operated came home to roost. Peter Bavasi recalls having a private dinner with Marvin Miller, founding director of the players' union, at the Post House in New York a few years after they had both retired from baseball. He remembers Miller as a brilliant and engaging fellow—as long as "you weren't battling him in a grievance arbitration." At the dinner, which Peter describes as very cordial, Miller told him:

> I don't think your father meant to deliver to us a four-part document that revealed how he and the other owners and general managers treated the players. But those *Sports Illustrated* articles

were better than any speech I could have made to the players. . . .
We arranged to have 40 copies of each of the articles delivered to
the home and visitors' clubhouses of each of the clubs, to ensure
that all active list players had a chance to read and discuss among
themselves what your father had said in print.

Years later, long into retirement, Buzzie struck up a correspondence with Miller. Peter Bavasi remembers seeing some
of the handwritten exchanges. "Buzz even wrote to a few of his
former colleagues on the Veterans Committee (before it was
reconfigured), recommending that they consider Marvin's candi-
dacy (for the Baseball Hall of Fame)." This represents a remarkable generosity on Buzzie's part; he himself was never elected
to the Hall. Hall of Fame admittance is the most subjective of
criteria. On the player side, sportswriters take a vote, and if
75 percent believe a person should be in the Hall, that player
is elected. There is also a Veterans Committee—the Historical
Overview Committee—that votes on baseball managers, executives, umpires, etc. By any reasonable standard Buzzie Bavasi
should be in the Hall of Fame. There are four GMs in the Hall
of Fame; three of them worked for the New York Yankees (Larry
MacPhail, Ed Barrow, and George Weiss). To reward someone
for being GM of the Yankees in the first part of the twentieth
century is akin to rewarding the managers of Bell Telephone
from 1920 to 1960 for continued success; in many ways, they
had a monopoly. The fourth GM in the Hall is Branch Rickey,
whose innovations are unquestionable. But as noted above, it
was Bavasi who finally brought Brooklyn a world championship.
And it was Bavasi who guided the Dodgers from one coast to
the other, winning another three World Series along the way. So
for Buzzie to write on behalf of an adversary like Marvin Miller
was really an extraordinary gesture.

The Bull, on the other hand, was a living poster child in 1966
for the freedom and agency of free agency that he would never
see during his own career. He was trapped on a world championship team behind a bevy of talented outfielders, unable to offer

his services to any other team. Had free agency existed in his time, Ferrara could have easily signed on with another, less talented, team, for presumably a higher salary and, more important to him, more playing time. As it was, he was a Dodger, and true to form, he launched into the 1966 season with the highest of hopes.

1966 and Beyond   **11**

The year 1966 became the first one in which Al Ferrara stayed in the Major Leagues for the entire season. He got into sixty-three games and batted .270. It was a good year for the Bull, moving into the Blair House midseason and getting to know the regulars there; they ranged from Richard Kiley of *Man of La Mancha* fame to the out-of-town strippers who worked at the Classic Cat strip club. He persuaded the owner of the Blair House to hire Herman Levy as a valet and doorman, although it was a mismatch of whatever talents Levy had. Richard Kiley casually left his car to be parked, and Levy promptly crushed a fender.

One of the Bull's duties included a monthly lunch with a charming woman in her eighties, Corinne Griffith. After growing up in Texas, she had come to Hollywood and became a silent movie star, been nominated for an Academy Award, and had been given the nickname "the Orchid Lady of the Screen." Her voice didn't translate well into talkies, and she turned to writing and marriage. Her third of four marriages was to Washington Redskins owner George Preston Marshall, and she wrote the lyrics to the Redskins' fight song, "Hail to the Redskins." Her memoir, *Papa's Delicate Condition*, became a best seller, and she followed it up with various books of recipes, screeds against taxation, and (in 1964) a book titled *Truth Is Stranger*, a title that certainly applied to her final marriage. Just before the Bull began having his monthly lunches with her, Corinne had quickly married and divorced her fourth husband, actor

Danny Scholl, who was twenty-five years younger than she. In court Griffith made the bizarre claim that she was actually her younger sister, who had taken Corinne's place upon her death. Two actresses who had been friends for decades testified that this was not true; Corinne was indeed Corinne, but in court Griffith stoutly maintained her story. If age is truly just a number, she refused to do the math and chose to present herself to the world as eternally a quarter century younger than she actually was. Ferrara found her a charming lunch companion, and certainly her love of storytelling fit right into the world of baseball with its endless supply of fables.

The 1966 season, in retrospect, was the Augustan Age of 1960s Dodgers baseball—the decline had begun, but there remained a golden sheen around the club. No one could tell that a year later the downfall would be complete. Koufax had perhaps his best season, winning another Cy Young award. Drysdale had an off year, but reliever Phil Regan was remarkable, going 14-1 and saving twenty-one games. Midway through the season someone gave the Bull a sombrero. He brought it into the clubhouse, and the Dodgers won. He put it on after the game as a sort of celebration, and the next night the team won again, with Ferrara again wearing the sombrero postgame. The team was going on a road trip, and Walter Alston told the Bull to bring the sombrero. It became a good luck totem for the rest of the season. When Koufax won his twentieth game, the Bull, wearing the sombrero, was photographed next to Koufax. The president of Mexico somehow heard about this tradition and sent Ferrara fifty sombreros. "What am I gonna do with 50 sombreros?" Al asks. "So of course I'm giving them out to the guys for their kids." As the season came down to the close, the pennant race tightened up. Ferrara had played on and off all year long, but his sombreros, and the general upbeat feeling he provided, were a constant. Ron Fairly remembers Ferrara for qualities tangible and intangible:

Al was a tough out. He was good at working pitchers, working a count. He was not a bad ball hitter, so a pitcher had to bring the ball close, and if the ball was close but not to Al's liking, he'd foul it off and make the pitcher throw another . . . and another. All that helps to wear down the pitcher. Whether or not he was in the lineup, he would study the pitcher from the dugout—"Can he get his curve ball over today? Is he up in the strike zone?" He was always ready whenever he was called on to hit. And he kept a lot of guys nice and loose. He was a damn good teammate.

Tommy Davis recalls Ferrara as a "funny dude. Couldn't have had a better teammate. He would liven up the bench—'Let's get going, goddamn it; you're making all this money; let's go.'" And Wes Parker identified Al as "confident—very confident; intelligent. He had the ability to focus himself, and he could rise to the occasion."

The 1966 season was a long grind. Maury Wills's legs took another beating; he twisted a knee during the season, and the pain plagued him throughout the year. Tommy Davis was still recovering from his cataclysmic leg injury. Koufax's arm ached every day. It was as if the exhaustion of five years of winning pennants and World Series and contending every single day had depleted the players of emotional and physical reserves. And hanging over their heads was a postseason goodwill tour of Japan. The goodwill was all on the part of Walter O'Malley. He had organized baseball's first tour of Japan following World War II. During that maiden tour of 1956, the expectation was that the Dodgers could easily win every game, and when they dropped one to the Tokyo Giants, Carl Erskine remembered that O'Malley read the team the riot act. He ended his rant by saying, "I know this is a goodwill tour and I want you to be gentlemen. . . . However, when you put on that Dodger uniform, I want you to remember Pearl Harbor." The 1956 trip was a success, and O'Malley was convinced that at some point in the future Major League baseball could expand into Japan. He planned a second trip following the 1966 season; he scheduled the team to depart on October 22 and play eighteen games. It was asking Dodger regulars to extend a long and exhausting season. O'Malley was paying each player $4,000 for the tour, a separate agreement from their regular baseball duties. Buzzie Bavasi, with some foresight, had declared that he was unable to go on the tour—he wanted no part of it. Drysdale and Koufax opted out; they had proved their power at the beginning of the season. Needing a star for the trip, O'Malley insisted that Maury Wills go. Wills pleaded with O'Malley: his legs were a mess; his knee had never recovered from a sprain; he was exhausted. O'Malley persisted, and Wills eventually relented but asked that his duties be restricted to goodwill ambassador—making appearances, signing autographs, and playing very little. He was assured that would be the case. Thus the seeds of disaster were planted during the summer. The unfortunate harvest would come in the fall.

The long 1966 season came down to the final day, with the Giants and Dodgers yet again locked in a tight pennant race. The Dodgers ended their season in Philadelphia with a three-game series. They lost to the Phillies on Friday night, and then Saturday's game was rained out. They would play a doubleheader on Sunday and needed just one win—or a Giant loss on Sunday—to clinch the pennant. On Saturday night the Bull and his new roommate, Bob Miller—Podres had been traded to the Tigers early in the season—decided to go to one of their favorite Philly haunts: the Sinatrama Room at the Latimer Cafe. It was a shrine to Frank, with wall-to-wall posters and Sinatra music playing continuously. Miller and Ferrara were already feeling celebratory. Drysdale was starting the first game of the doubleheader, giving the Dodgers excellent prospects. If for some reason they didn't win that game, they had Koufax for the second game. They couldn't lose. The World Series would start in Los Angeles, and Ferrara figured the team would need some alcohol for the flight back. He organized a kitty and purchased assorted beverages. The next day Miller and the Bull smuggled the case of hard liquor into the clubhouse, stashing it in Miller's locker.

As the doubleheader started, the Dodger dugout got updates from Pittsburgh, where the Giants were playing the Pirates.

The game went into extra innings, and the Giants won. On their end the Dodgers took a 3–2 lead into the eighth inning. Drysdale had been off from the start—the Phillies had tagged him for four hits and two runs in the first two innings—and Walter Alston put in Ron Perranoski. Then two innings later he called to the bullpen for Bob Miller. Miller had not anticipated this situation, but he was game. He worked two scoreless innings, but in the eighth the Phillies' Dick Allen got an infield single. Bill White bunted, and Miller misplayed the ball, overthrowing first base. Allen moved to third and White to second. Alston called for his ace reliever, Phil Regan, to come in. He intentionally walked Dick Groat, bringing up Cookie Rojas. Rojas grounded to third—but the usually sure-handed Dick Schofield made an error on his throw to first. A run scored. Two errors in the inning, and now the game was tied. The next batter, catcher Clay Dalrymple, singled to center, and the Phillies led, 4–3. That was the ball game. The Dodgers went down one-two-three in the top of the ninth.

In between games Buzzie Bavasi stormed down to the clubhouse. This was unheard of; GMs don't intrude on a clubhouse in general but especially not between the two games of a doubleheader. Buzzie was furious. He marched to Miller's locker, where the booze was stashed. Somehow he knew a stash of Johnny Walker had been smuggled in. He knew everything that went on through some mysterious process of information osmosis that filtered through the clubhouse attendants, the coaches, and the bat boys. He roared, "You sons of bitches, what are you doing? You want to have a celebration, I'll show you a celebration." He smashed the bottles and left, furious. The Dodgers were down to their final game of the season and now had to turn to Koufax.

The Giants were already in the Pittsburgh airport, and a reporter asked pitcher Ron Herbel if the team knew where it was headed. He replied, "We know where we're going. No way Superman loses the second game." Koufax didn't. He pitched eight shutout innings; the Dodgers scored six runs; and although the Phillies scored three runs and threatened in the ninth, he struck out two of the final three batters to win the game and the pennant. No one knew it at the time, but it was the last game he would win.

The Dodgers' celebration after the game was subdued, and not just because their hard alcohol had literally gone down the drain. They were exhausted. The players boarded their flight home. They stopped in St. Louis, and there was a desperate attempt for a liquor run. A clubhouse man was dispatched to buy whatever he could, but they had forgotten Missouri's blue laws. The state sold only near beer on Sundays, so the second half of the flight was lightly toasted, and they landed in Los Angeles, once again pennant winners and completely sober. But now the mighty Dodger engine, the team that ran on nerves of steel, sputtered to a halt. The World Series was against a Baltimore Orioles team that featured pitchers Jim Palmer, Dave McNally, Moe Drabowsky, and the little-heralded Wally Bunker. Of those four pitchers three threw shutouts. The Dodgers scored single runs in the second and third innings of the opening game and didn't score a run for the rest of the series. Koufax started Game Two and was hurt by the infamous fifth inning. Poor Willie Davis committed three errors in the inning, and three runs scored. Ferrara, and knowledgeable baseball people, knew Davis as a reliable center fielder; it was the only time that the Bull recalls Davis's playing poorly in the field. But it happened on a national stage at a crucial moment (the game had been scoreless until the fifth), and that inning is as indelible in Dodger fans' minds as a water mark on a pristine ceiling when the name "Willie Davis" is mentioned.

The Dodgers lost both of the final two games, 1–0. It was perhaps a fitting conclusion to the era of nerves of steel—two games with just two runs scored. The Dodgers finished the series with a stretch of thirty-three scoreless innings. In the top of the ninth inning in Baltimore, with one out and the Dodgers trailing, Ferrara was called upon to pinch-hit. The Bull finally got up to hit in a World Series. He faced Dave McNally and hit a solid single to center. The man who defined fearlessness came through in the clutch. Nate Oliver pinch-ran for him, and then Maury Wills walked. That represented the potential winning run. Willie Davis came up with a chance to redeem himself for Game Two—but lined out to right field. And the final hope, Sweet Lou Johnson, flew out to center. The Dodgers' run was over.

After that game the Dodgers flew back to Los Angeles, and Ferrara sat next to Koufax on the plane. The Bull started talking about the offseason and plans for next year when Koufax interrupted him. "This is it," Sandy said. Ferrara sat back. He didn't push Koufax further. Sandy was telling the truth, and the Bull heard it. Sandy was going to retire. Ferrara knew that Koufax had confided in him with his typical restraint and elegance. The Bull had information that was the scoop of the century, but he told no one. He knew that Koufax would let the world know in his own time and manner.

And then the exhausted team headed for Japan. The players were given their $4,000 payment in cash when they arrived. Handing young baseball players, including men like Al Ferrara, $4,000 in cash would seem like an invitation for disaster. Sure enough, the Bull's good friend Don Zimmer, who spent sixty-five years in professional baseball playing throughout the Minor and Major Leagues and coaching and managing various teams, needed a loan of $500 almost immediately, and the Bull provided it. Then Jim Brewer quickly had his cash stolen from him, and the team pooled money to help him get through the tour. As a result, Ferrara was out $700 almost from the start of the trip. But he was always happy to explore new cultures, and he quickly bonded with a Japanese woman named Ei at a hostess club. He communicated with her through the ad hoc international sign language he had mastered in the Caribbean and managed to convey, "What do you want to do after we leave here? Do I have to give you money to get you out of here?" She blurted out something he couldn't understand, and he got closer to her and eventually realized she was saying, "Corn soup." She wanted a bowl of corn soup. The Bull had never had corn soup: "My mother made tomato soup; what's with this corn soup, you know?" But he took Ei out for corn soup, tried it, liked it, and they retired to a Western-style hotel, with beds instead of the usual tatami mats and bedding for floor sleeping. During the tour of Japan the Bull and Ei were constant companions, with the exception of a night in Hiroshima, where the hotel offered massages. The Bull was rooming with third baseman John Kennedy (who was extremely popular in Japan just because he shared his name with the late president), and Kennedy burst out laughing when he saw what the Japanese massage featured. The Bull recalls: "She says, turn over, and I turned over, and she stands up on my back and starts running, running up and down my back on her feet; it was no hand massage. But it was the most wonderful thing I ever felt."

The Bull was enjoying his trip, but for Maury Wills it was agony. Instead of being a goodwill ambassador, shaking hands and posing for pictures, he was called upon to play every day. His knee got worse, particularly after a game played on an entirely dirt infield in Sapporo. Running to second base, Wills twisted his knee badly and told Walter Alston he was hurt. Then Wills, who was the team captain, decided he had to leave the tour for the sake of his health. He got on a plane and stopped in Hawaii. Wills always had his banjo with him; he enjoyed playing and performing, and his musicality proved to be the end of his road with the Dodgers. Entertainer Don Ho asked him to play a few songs with him at Ho's nightclub in Oahu. Photos were taken that appeared in the press. Wills looked as if he had claimed an injury but then ended up vacationing in Hawaii instead of getting medical treatment. When the team returned from Japan, O'Malley instructed Buzzie to trade the team's captain. Buzzie Bavasi, like the players in his charge, had a master to answer to. O'Malley paid the bills, so Bavasi set about figuring out a trade. But the impending trade of Wills was only the second most significant shock to the Dodgers in November. On November 18, while the team and its owner were in Japan, Sandy Koufax called a press conference and announced his retirement.

In the *Sports Illustrated* series Buzzie details his attempts to get Koufax to wait until the team returned from Japan to make the announcement, but, in classic Koufax fashion, Sandy had told one sportswriter in complete confidence that he was going to retire and insisted on honoring the commitment to an exclusive scoop when it looked as though the news was going to break. Combined with the subsequent trade of Maury Wills, Koufax's retirement effectively ended the nerves-of-steel era.

So the Dodgers launched into the 1967 season without both their captain and the best pitcher in history. In the winter of 1966 the Bull himself decided to call a press conference. He gathered together sportswriters and made a dramatic announcement: no matter how much the Dodgers pleaded, he would *not* play shortstop. It made headlines, of course, and offered a bit of levity to break up the bleak news facing the Dodgers. That same winter Buzzie sent out the contracts as usual, and the Bull didn't sign his. Buzzie called him up and asked him what the problem was. The Bull said he needed more money. Buzzie replied, "If you weren't playing baseball, what would you do? What do you think you'd do if you don't sign that contract and have to find another job?" The Bull replied, "I've got it all figured out. I'm going to open a detective agency. Private eye." Buzzie laughed. "No, I'm serious," Al continued. "I'm really going to do this. I've even got the name: The Bull's Eye." They both cracked up, and the Bull signed the deal.

In 1967 the mighty Dodger dynasty finally collapsed. Without Koufax and Wills the team ended up in eighth place in the National League, 28 1/2 games behind the league-leading Cardinals. For Buzzie a losing season was both a rarity and a plague. Since he had been named GM in 1950 for the 1951 season, the Dodgers had never finished this poorly. The 1967 season crawled to an end as the Dodgers beat the hapless New York Mets at Dodger Stadium. The team was dressing in the locker room and getting ready to eat a special buffet. There was chatter and laughter; the long dismal season was finally over. Bavasi walked into the clubhouse, strode to the folding table laden with food, and hurled it over. "We'll see how many of you are here next year," he burst out. Buzzie was intensely competitive; the idea of finding any laughter or joy in the miserable 1967 season was beyond him. Ironically it would be Bavasi himself who would be gone by the end of 1968.

But if the year was terrible for the Dodgers, 1967 was also the year Ferrara finally broke through. He proved that given the chance to play a full season, he could produce on a par with the best of Major Leaguers. He led the team in home runs with sixteen, was second in RBIS, batted .277 in 122 games, and was named the most valuable Dodger by the Los Angeles sportswriters. Had he been on another club in the previous three years, he probably would have been a starter and put up similar numbers. Fifty years later Ferrara assesses how he feels: "Back then, in the 1960s, I would rather have played. But now—I'll take the World Series championships."

In addition, Al's occasional acting career blossomed. Lee Walls, who had played for a variety of teams including the 1963 Dodgers, had become a talent manager. Hollywood was thrilled with the mid-1960s Dodgers and ready to cast them in any number of roles. Part of Koufax and Drysdale's leverage during the 1966 holdout, after all, had been that they had a movie deal. Ferrara's first opportunity came on *Gilligan's Island*. He and fellow Dodger Jim Lefebvre were cast against type, shall we say, as native headhunters in an episode titled "High Man on the Totem Pole." Today there would be protesters lined up on Radford Avenue in Studio City (where *Gilligan's Island* was shot), indicting show creator Sherwood Schwartz for numerous counts of insensitivity, but at the time it was a lark for the Bull and Lefebvre to don war paint and grass skirt costumes and carry machetes as they threatened Thurston Howell III and his wife.

One of the producers of the hit TV show *Batman*, Howie Horwitz, was a huge Dodger fan who had seats right behind home plate. He befriended Ferrara and hired him for several episodes. The Bull appeared as "Atlas" with Zsa Gabor, who played the role of Minerva, spa owner and jewel thief. (Gabor was very nice to Ferrara but ordered one female player to be fired because she insisted, as the Bull recalls, "No one can be blonder than me.") The Bull also had the honor of acting alongside Tallulah Bankhead on two other *Batman* episodes. Bankhead played the Black Widow, and Ferrara was her henchman, "Trap Door." He was a vivid presence, placing an enormous spider on Batman, who was enmeshed in a huge spiderweb. Viewing at home, Al's grandmother relayed to him that "she was annoyed that Robin knocked me on my ass," but such is the fate of the actor. Ferrara was riding high that offseason, holding court at the Blair House, hobnobbing with Hollywood celebrities, and looking forward to a new baseball season. As the 1968 season started, the Bull had finally established himself as a valuable power-hitting outfielder.

In the winter of 1967–68 Buzzie suggested a salary strategy to Ferrara. He would pay him $26,000, but $5,000 of that would be held until after the season. That way Ferrara would know he'd have something to live on during the offseason. The assumption— which they both shared—was that the Bull would blow through whatever money he made during the year. Being the grasshopper instead of the ant, he would enter the winter broke. Buzzie and Ferrara had tried a variant of this strategy once before: Ferrara had agreed to have $1,000 of his salary each month put in a savings account from which it couldn't be withdrawn without Buzzie's approval. At the end of the season he'd have $6,000. When the season ended, Buzzie instructed the bank to release the money. Unfortunately there was no money. On the first of every month the Bull had borrowed $1,000 against the money in the account, and it was all gone. The two agreed to try it again in 1968. But the actual contract would be for only $21,000. The additional $5,000 was a handshake deal. Ferrara signed. What neither man could predict was that Buzzie would be gone by the end of the year—and without anything on paper the Dodgers would refuse to pay the additional $5,000.

Thursday, April 11, was the second game of the Dodgers' season. Ferrara was playing left field. In the top of the eighth inning

Tommy Agee of the New York Mets hit a sinking line drive to left. The Bull, aggressive as always, charged the ball. As he dove to try to make the catch, his leg twisted out from under him. His left ankle snapped. It was completely turned around. He was taken to Daniel Freeman Hospital, and Buzzie's good friend, Dr. Robert Kerlan, came and did an examination. He told Ferrara that he could approach resetting it in one of two ways: either in the traditional fashion, a more gentle approach, which would take many months to mend, or "Vietnam War style," a quick and brutal snap to get the bones back in alignment. Ferrara opted for the latter approach. Kerlan snapped the ankle back into alignment; the pain was excruciating, but it worked. Nonetheless, the Bull's season was over. More than that, it was the last time he would play for the Los Angeles Dodgers.

Up in the front office Buzzie Bavasi began the 1968 season looking into his future with the Dodger organization. He saw something inevitable approaching: Walter O'Malley's son Peter had worked his way through the organization, from director of Dodgertown to GM at Spokane to vice-president in charge of stadium operations. It seemed clear that his father would hand the real running of the ball club over to his son at some point in time. Then Bavasi got a golden opportunity: Major League baseball decided to add four expansion teams for the 1969 season. One of them was to be in San Diego, owned by local businessman C. Arnholt Smith, and Buzzie was offered a chance to become part owner and president of the team. Before the end of the 1968 season—another losing year for the Dodgers—Buzzie announced his plans. He had intended to stay through the season, but Walter O'Malley (who was supportive of Buzzie's decision) wanted him to resign immediately, presumably to get his salary off the payroll. So Buzzie resigned and moved south.

Having missed the 1968 season, Ferrara was dispatched to Arizona in the fall to get back into playing shape in the Instructional League. On the same team was his old buddy Johnny Podres, now hoping to hang on to the remainder of a Major League career. One day they both got a surprising call: Buzzie Bavasi was selecting players in the expansion draft, and toward the end of the process he decided to make his team fun and chose two old favorites in the expansion draft: Podres and the Bull. The two rounders were reunited, and they were thrilled.

In January 1969 Buzzie called Ferrara down to San Diego. He had a proposal: he wanted to hire Ferrara and sportswriter Bud Tucker to do advance work on behalf of the new team. They were going to be goodwill ambassadors for the Padres, circulating through the community, making the rounds of Rotary Club lunches and Little League gatherings. On the very first day of this employment Al and Tucker decided to celebrate their new jobs. They began their promotional work at a bar and grew incredibly happy with the future of the team. They decided to continue their goodwill tour at another bar, and Tucker got behind the wheel. As he drove onto the highway, police lights flashed behind him. He pulled over, weaving as he went, and within minutes the police had him under arrest for driving under the influence. They handcuffed Tucker—and then handcuffed the Bull. "Wait, I wasn't driving—what did I do?" Al asked. The years have obscured the charges, but both Tucker and the Bull found themselves on day one of their jobs having to call Buzzie Bavasi from the police lockup, asking for bail money.

Everything about the Padres was different from the Dodgers. Buzzie cut a deal for their spring training site in Yuma, Arizona, a small town near the Mexican border whose most notable attraction was a dog track. A local group known as the Caballeros had lured the Padres with an all-expense-paid facility, a $20,000 cash bonus, and the promise of a new stadium in short order. Unlike in Dodgertown, with its multiple playing fields, there was just one in Yuma that first year—Keegan Field. The clubhouse was the public swimming pool's dressing room. Some of the personnel was the same—with his usual loyalty Buzzie had hired old Dodger hands like Herman Levy and John Mattei. On the first day of spring training the Bull asked

Mattei for a second towel, and Mattei replied, "That's it. You only get one towel. We can't afford any more." Such was life with the Padres. Buzzie Bavasi quickly found out that C. Arnholt Smith was playing with borrowed money. And some of that was Buzzie's. At one point Buzzie put his own home up as surety for the Padres' financial position. As the season started and it quickly became apparent that the team was scrambling to pay its bills, Buzzie became more and more anxious. He was forced to trade players not to improve the team but just to get enough cash to make payroll.

In 1969 and 1970 the Bull played more games than at any other point in his career. Each season he got in 138 games, batted .260 and .277, and hit thirteen and fourteen home runs in a pitcher-friendly ballpark. Although his broken ankle had slowed him down, he showed what he could do as a regular Major League player. Al was romancing a blonde at the time; she made the mistake of sharing her bank account with the Bull as he wagered on the horses. The account was soon empty, and she went to—who else?—Buzzie Bavasi to complain. She shared with him something that the Bull had said in front of her eight-year-old daughter the night before; it involved dropping the "F" bomb. Buzzie asked her to return the next day with the Bull. They came to his office, and the blonde turned to the Bull. "Tell Mr. Bavasi what you said to me in front of my daughter two nights ago."

"What do you mean?" Ferrara asked.

"You told me to go piss in my hat."

"Don't talk that way in front of Buzzie!"

In the end Buzzie wrote out a check for the $2,000, an amount that she had fronted the Bull, and he told her to move somewhere else. Three days later they were back together.

For Buzzie the serious financial pressure came not from the Bull's shenanigans but from those of the Padres' owner. Within two years the team was on the verge of bankruptcy. Later it would be revealed that C. Arnholt Smith had not only misrepresented his deep pockets, but he was also actually a criminal. He had built his fortune through ownership of the United States National Bank in San Diego; it failed in October 1973 because it had loaned excessive amounts of money to companies that Smith controlled. Smith pled no contest to bank fraud charges in 1975, and in 1979 he was convicted of embezzling over eight million dollars, part of which involved his eventual sale of the Padres. Buzzie was trying to navigate a new team through all this. No one knew at the time of Buzzie's distress, either personal or financial, as he was forced to deal away players to make payroll.

The 1970 season ended painfully for the Bull. In one of the last games of the year he was hit by a pitch that struck him in the eye. He was hospitalized and missed the final few games. The Bull never assigns external blame—he always plays the hand he has been dealt—but his hitting never rebounded.

Early in the 1971 season Buzzie made a trade he wished he had never had to make: he dealt away Ferrara to the Cincinnati Reds. In exchange the Padres received Angel Bravo, a marginal player from Venezuela who ended up batting .248 over three seasons in the big leagues. More significant, the Padres received $35,000 cash. Buzzie didn't tell the Bull at the time, but he needed it to make that month's payroll.

Ferrara reported promptly to the Reds. His life had been complicated by a relationship with a woman in San Diego who was reluctant to pick up and move to Ohio, especially without any formal commitment, so the Bull arranged for a hasty wedding. (The marriage ultimately fell apart.) He was saddened to leave Bavasi and Southern California, but as always, he moved forward.

Al was immediately placed in left field. In his very first game for the Reds a fly ball sailed out to him. Attempting to field it, the Bull says he "looked like a turtle wrestling a football." After the inning was over Ferrara jogged to the dugout. Manager Sparky Anderson was resting his arms on the dugout railing, glaring at him. The Bull looked to him and immediately said, "What did you expect for Angel Bravo—Willie Mays?"

The Bull's time with Cincinnati did not go particularly well. He played sporadically, did not hit well, and roomed with up-and-coming superstar Johnny Bench. Bench was besieged by legions of female fans. Ferrara was the last person to disparage affection, but as he struggled to save his career, the phone ringing off the hook in hotel rooms they shared night after night tired him out. He asked Bench to have the hotels' front desks hold his calls, but out of some excessive sense of courtesy or opportunity, Bench wanted to answer the phone. The Bull missed Buzzie. No other GM had the sort of personal relationship that Buzzie had with his players, and the cultural change from a Bavasi system to a typical Major League management system was a shock. Some of the Reds players got involved in a basketball tournament during the offseason. Even though the Reds urged them not to do so because of a fear of injury, they played, and Ferrara joined them. He was the one the Reds management griped about—not their superstars on the team. It was the old story of a double standard; superstars could lead their own lives, but players on the bubble were expected to tow the company line.

At the end of the season Reds vice-president Sheldon "Chief" Bender (a veteran Reds executive not to be confused with the Hall of Fame Native American pitcher Chief Bender of an earlier era) called the Bull. He told him the Reds were sending his contract to their AAA Minor League team in Indianapolis. Ferrara asked, "Why don't you give me my release?" That way he could sign on with another Major League team. Bender replied the Reds had an investment in Ferrara.

"Well," said the Bull, "I'm not going to Indy."

"We don't want you there," said Bender. "We aren't going to release you until Indianapolis goes to spring training. See if you can find another team that will spend $16,000 on you."

Essentially Chief Bender and the Reds were asking Ferrara to do their front-office work for them. He was tasked with finding another team to take over his contract. It was a penurious and degrading maneuver from an organization that had a reputation of being tightfisted and unrelenting. Ferrara sent telegrams to every Major League club. He got three responses—from old friends Ken Aspromonte at Cleveland (who had grown up in the same Brooklyn neighborhood), Leo Durocher at the Cubs, and Frank Lucchesi with the Phillies. They all said they loved him, but they couldn't use him.

Desperate to hang on, the Bull called the owner of the Hawaii Islanders in the Pacific Coast League. They struck a verbal deal: when Ferrara got his release, he could come to Hawaii and play. Major League teams reported to spring training on March 1, but Ferrara was no longer on the Major League roster, so he had to wait for the Minor League team to report in order to get his official release. Finally toward the end of March, the Reds released him. He called the Hawaii Islanders, and the GM told him he was sorry, but they had just signed Lee May for that slot.

"I was left with a sour taste about a game that I loved," Ferrara sighs. "I was the off-the-field character. When the time comes for guys like me, you're gone. They laughed with you, but if you can't do anything for them on the field, you're gone." Ferrara likened the experience to the moment when his mother passed away: "I go to school one day, I come home from class, and my mother is gone. Final, quick; [she had] moved on. Baseball: I'm planning on playing in Hawaii, [but] a guy tells me, 'Tough; it's over.' No chance any more—I'm out. It's final. It's final in other words—the two loves in my life. My mother and baseball. They were never going to be any more."

The Bull was marooned in Ohio. A consummate big city guy, a native of Brooklyn, and the toast of Los Angeles, he was now exiled to the environs of Cincinnati while he pondered his next move. He muses: "One of my big statements that I've made since I was a young man whenever . . . there were catastrophes looming all over was, 'Relax, don't panic,' and then I would relax. . . . I find myself to be an amusing question-and-answer person. . . . I can ask myself a question and get a pretty good answer." The Bull came up with a "pretty good answer": Covington, Kentucky. Right across the river from Cincinnati, together with neighboring Newport, it had a storied history as the Sin City of Kentucky. It was littered with dozens of brothels and illicit gambling dens, and virtually every bar offered a chance to gamble. The place was full of bookies taking wagers on nearby horse tracks. The Bull checked into the YMCA and got his bearings. He quickly discovered the Shamrock Bar.

The Shamrock was populated by the kind of outsized characters that seemed to follow Ferrara wherever he was. It was owned by a loud, assertive woman with brilliant red hair named Rusty, and there were regulars like a woman nicknamed Sea Biscuit (thanks to her equine face), Coupon Eddy, and a woman who would become a familiar companion, Peppermint Patty. Coupon Eddy stood on the corner in front of the Shamrock every day, selling five-dollar coupons for discounted photos. The moment he made a sale, he would take the five dollars, come into the Shamrock, and spend the entire day there on his new income. He would place a two-dollar bet on a horse race and a two-dollar bet on the numbers game, and he would save a dollar for the bartender's tip. People at the bar would buy him drinks all day long, and he would talk out of the side of his mouth in a distinctive New York accent, advising everyone, "If you're going to be a sucker, be a quiet one." He also had advice for the Bull: "Let me tell you something, son: never check into that YMCA where you're living now. That shows your position. Never check into the YMCA." The Bull took his advice and moved into a little apartment near Coupon Eddy's place. He also somehow talked Rusty into hiring him as a bartender. While he had consumed plenty of drinks, he had never mixed one—but now he was tending bar. Rusty offered him some advice: "Everyone steals from a bar. Just keep it reasonable." Within half a year he had developed an affection for Covington and its wide-open ways. Latonia race track was a centerpiece of the community, and one could place a bet anywhere in town. Peppermint Patty was a pleasant companion, and he enjoyed the companionship offered by Rusty and the Shamrock patrons.

As the Bull was navigating a strange new life in Covington, Kentucky, Buzzie Bavasi was trying to survive the criminal inept-

itude of the Padres' principal owner. When C. Arnholt Smith
launched his bid for the expansion team, Bavasi anticipated that
the cost to get into the National League would be seven million
dollars. When it turned out the bill was ten million, Bavasi advised
Smith to back out because Smith wouldn't have enough money to
operate the club properly. Smith got the franchise anyway, and
then every expenditure became a tortured transaction. Buzzie
had the chance to sign future star Doug DeCinces, but DeCinces
asked for a $6,000 signing bonus in order to pay for college. The
Padres had only $4,000, so because they couldn't offer an addi-
tional $2,000, they lost a core player.

Buzzie and the Bull, two old friends, now shared a kind of exile
from the promised land. The Bull was cut off from the world of
baseball, tending bar at the Shamrock, pouring drinks for Coupon Eddy and Sea Biscuit; Buzzie was scraping together payrolls
for a swindler. It was now 1971, and the turmoil in America that
had peaked in 1968—with the assassinations of Martin Luther
King Jr. and Robert Kennedy, the height of the Vietnam War, and
the election of Richard Nixon—had cooled down. The passionate drive for excellence that had framed the 1965 baseball season,
the year when Buzzie demanded nerves of steel from his entire
team, had now become a fight for survival. C. Arnholt Smith had
been a civic fixture in San Diego for over thirty years, but with
the Padres failing, he cut a deal to move the team to Washington
DC. The moving trucks were in place when suddenly San Diego
and Buzzie were rescued: Ray Kroc, the principal shareholder of
McDonald's, came in with an offer of ten million dollars to buy
the team. Buzzie had never heard of Kroc; when he first asked
who Kroc was, he assumed he owned the McDonnell Douglas Air-
craft Company. Peter Bavasi corrected his father's misimpres-
sion, Kroc made the deal, and the Padres—and Buzzie—stayed
in San Diego. One of Kroc's first actions was to pay Bavasi back
for the personal loan he had made to the team. Buzzie's financial nightmare was over.

Following the 1972 season Buzzie had promoted his son Peter
to be the Padres' GM. Peter promptly showed his baseball savvy

by drafting future Hall of Famer Dave Winfield in the 1973 draft. The Kroc era officially began in 1974. When Peter left the Padres to become the president of the expansion Toronto Blue Jays, Buzzie and Peter became the first father and son to be the chief executives of Major League baseball teams at the same time.

If Buzzie had found a savior in Ray Kroc, the Bull needed a savior after a couple of years in Covington. He found himself in the uncomfortable position of needing to cover a horse-racing debt and not having the means to do so. His instinct was that he had to get out of town—fast. But how? And where would he go? He turned to his old friend Bobby T—Bobby Tarzia, Al's close childhood friend in Brooklyn and now a Los Angeleno running a hair salon. Bobby T paid for a plane ticket for Al to come to Los Angeles, and Ferrara crashed on his couch in West Los Angeles. Bobby was an excellent cook; the Bull knew that if nothing else, he would eat well; but then Tarzia decided he was getting a little heavy and went on a popular diet of the time, the pasta diet. For six months Ferrara ate pasta and scraped along, trying to figure out what he could do. He decided that he could return to a scene of earlier glory—Reno, Nevada—and was on the verge of moving there to go to card-dealing school when he had lunch with Joe Blanchard. Blanchard had lived at Blair House during the Bull's run there and was an agent for bands, booking them into clubs on the Sunset Strip. When Ferrara told him he was moving to Reno, Blanchard wisely said, "What are you going to Reno for? You're a Dodger, man; they remember you in Los Angeles." He then proceeded to walk across the street to the Marquis Restaurant, run by Mario Marino, who knew Ferrara from his patronage of his previous restaurant. Mario welcomed the Bull with open arms—a fellow Italian— asked how he was doing, and (when he heard of Al's plan to move to Reno) quickly proposed an alternative: be the maitre d' at his restaurant. "I said I don't even know what side the fork goes on," Al admitted. "I can't open a bottle of wine; I don't know anything." Mario replied, "Don't worry." He pulled one hundred dollars out of the cash register, handed it to Ferrara, and said, "Go get yourself a tuxedo. Be in here at five o'clock tonight. You got the job."

Thus began a new act for the Bull, ruling the Marquis as its resident maitre d'. He never tossed a salad and never poured a bottle of wine, but he acted as a consummate conductor of the orchestra that comprised the restaurant's symphony. He greeted guests and steered them into appropriate seating. There was a White Room for the high-level celebrities that frequented the Marquis, such as Frank Sinatra or Steve Lawrence and Eydie Gormé. The piano bar had its regulars, and he directed traffic in and out of the bar and greeted everyone at the door like a long-lost friend. He was always dressed in a tuxedo, which he wore on the bus ride over to the Marquis—he still didn't drive. The Bull became a fixture on the Sunset Strip. He started seeing the well-known stripper Liberty West (her stage name), and eventually they moved in together. She was frequently on the road, and their apartment became the home base for parties—a kind of 1970s version of the Mayfair. Screenwriter Frank Ray Perilli got Ferrara roles in two films: *Dracula's Dog* and *Mansion of the Doomed*. In the latter film Al got to appear with distinguished actors Richard Basehart and Gloria Grahame in an otherwise undistinguished horror movie that revolved around an insane surgeon abducting people and removing their eyeballs in an attempt to transplant them into his daughter, who had lost her own in a car accident he had caused. The memorable tag line on the movie's one-sheet read: "WHAT HAPPENS IS SO HORRIFYING WE CAN'T EVEN HINT AT IT IN THIS POSTER."

It was during this period that the Bull's remarkable constitution was perhaps weathering its greatest assault. Ferrara had never smoked until he got to the Major Leagues. Once a Dodger walked into the clubhouse, he was greeted with free cartons of Tareyton cigarettes. From zero Ferrara became a five-pack-a-day smoker. He had always enjoyed a drink, but now the combination of hosting what amounted to a nightly party at the Marquis, followed by an informal party at his apartment, found the Bull downing between eighteen and twenty-four scotch and sodas a night. It is remarkable that when the time eventually came some years later to quit these habits, Al was able to do so. One day he decided to stop smoking and quit cold turkey. He has been sober now for over thirty years, and with alcohol too, he simply stopped. The most difficult habit to quit, he found, was his daily ten cups of coffee. But he did so.

Al also stopped playing the field with women who had adorned his life. He met one woman, Kay Donno, who has been at his side for the past thirty years. She is a beautiful and gracious woman who has accompanied the Bull through his days as a maitre d'; through a third career in which the Bull sold a somewhat dubious home improvement product (a house coating treatment; Kay helped Ferrara put together a notebook of his days as a Dodger that sold prospective customers more on the Bull than the product); through a three-year stint in Las Vegas; and finally back to Los Angeles. During the period in which Ferrara was making a good living selling the home improvement product, Peter Bavasi called him up. He offered him a job as a hitting coach for the newly formed Toronto Blue Jays. Ferrara pondered the offer, but the salary was substantially less than he was making at the time. He turned it down, a decision that he says was "the right decision that was the wrong decision." Had he known how the salary base of Major League baseball was to grow, even for coaches, he would have taken the offer.

But the intersection of the Bavasi family and the Bull was not over. In 1977 Angels owner Gene Autry hired Buzzie as executive vice-president and general manager. Buzzie entered the new era of free agency in baseball and mastered it as he had mastered baseball's various other eras: the 1940s period of building extensive farm teams; the bonus baby decades; the pitching dominant 1960s. He invested in free agents like Reggie Jackson, Rod Carew, and Fred Lynn, and under Buzzie the Angels won the American League West division titles in 1979 and 1982. Finally, nearing seventy, Buzzie decided to retire, and 1984 was his last season as a baseball executive. His career had spanned

four decades—although one could say it really spanned at least
two more. He was on the phone virtually every day with his four
sons, offering advice and nudges. Three of them have remained
major figures in baseball: Peter was the founding president of
the Blue Jays and then GM of the Cleveland Indians and a mem-
ber of Major League Baseball's Executive Council. Bill was GM
of the Seattle Mariners and California Angels and now works in
Player Development for Major League Baseball. Bob, along with
his wife Margaret, owned a number of baseball-related endeavors,
including the Minor League Everett AquaSox. (The fourth son,
Chris, served as mayor of Flagstaff, Arizona, for seven terms.)

During all of these years the Bull and Buzzie maintained a
correspondence. With the advent of email they began exchang-
ing regular messages. When the financial crisis of 2008 hit, the
Bull was one of its casualties: his pension decreased by a quarter. Ferrara felt he "was buried. Who would hire a sixty-eight-
year-old man?" Peter Bavasi and Bob Case (former assistant
visiting clubhouse manager for the Dodgers) encouraged Ferrara to call the Dodgers and talk with them about becoming one
of the Dodger ambassadors. Case drove the Bull to Dodger Stadium, where he met with Dodger historian Mark Langill. Always
a great raconteur, Ferrara delighted Langill, who took him to
the press box to say hello to Vin Scully. The greeting, as Ferrara says, "was nothing short of sensational. We talked about
old times, we told stories of Vero Beach and the sixties and the
wonderful characters of that era, and he remarked that surely I
was one of those characters. I felt great. I felt like I was back in
the big leagues again." In short order, Ferrara was hired as an
ambassador for the Los Angeles Dodgers. He is reunited with
the team he has loved since childhood. He visits schools, Little
League fields, and veterans' hospitals all over the Los Angeles area,
offering inspirational talks, and he hosts clinics for young players at Dodger Stadium. Ferrara recalls that his very first assign-
ment was doing a kindergarten reading: "What was I going to
say to them? I thought of how I had hit point zero eight three in
high school; that's nothing to talk about. I had bartended with-

out ever mixing a drink. I had been a maître d without tossing a salad or opening a bottle of wine. I owned a home improvement company, not knowing a thing about putting a nail in the wall." But, he quickly realized, "I was a Dodger. Check your ego at the door; it's about them. Meet who you are talking to, look at the smiles, the twinkle in their eyes."

Al has reunited as a Dodger ambassador with old friends like Tommy Davis and Sweet Lou Johnson, and even now Ferrara feels the responsibility of a man who has to offer something more: "I was never a big star. So I have to be better. And the schools always ask for me to come back." He works tirelessly for LA Reads, a program of the Los Angeles Dodgers Foundation that encourages young children to read. He uses the metaphor of a baseball diamond in his talks:

> To be a success we have to touch home plate, but first we have to go around the bases, and almost all of us need help. Our parents help us get to first base; our schools and libraries help us get to second. At third base are our mentors, teachers, and coaches. And then we have to head to home plate. Some do this easy, some, like myself, kept stumbling along the way. I had my gal Kay to pick me up and the Dodgers to give me the opportunity to get there. I crawled home, but I got there.

Ferrara, seated at his little kitchen table in his Studio City apartment, breaks into a wide grin: "Who's getting himself home in life now? Me. This is me now, coming to home plate and touching it. I touched home plate. I got there. Not the big hit in a World Series, not the rings. I got there with this. I've done something. I feel good about it."

For eight years the Bull has been visiting Horace Mann Elementary in Glendale, California. It's a school where 97 percent of the students come from families that cannot afford to pay for a child's lunch. Ferrara was initially invited to reinforce the outlook of the school motto: "Do your best." He immediately won the kids over by talking with them—not at them—and doing so directly and honestly. He related how he worked himself up and applied himself to whatever situation was at hand. Teacher Specialist Chris Burt says of Ferrara,

> Our kids have a lot of issues. He just gives us the sense that he can do it, and if he can do it, [the child] can do it. And how? Simple: Do your best. Do your best and don't give up. He is a hero to so many of our kids. Even after a few minutes with some of them, he touched their lives. His message to us has consistently been that everyone is a part of the team. They are team players, and we are in this to win. He knows what it is to be a team player and win.

A thank you note from a South Pasadena grade school sums up the kind of joy the Bull brings now to school children all over Los Angeles:

> What a blessing you are! You are gifted with such a generous heart, and your eyes for each child (and each adult) are filled with great warmth and enthusiasm. . . . I was aware that you had played piano at Carnegie Hall, but when you spoke about telling your grandmother you had decided to play baseball, I was struck by how true it is that you obviously made the right choice. . . . You have extended your legacy beyond baseball to being an ambassador who inspires, delights and encourages the next generation.

Buzzie and Evit Bavasi lived by the ocean in La Jolla, California, never far from the world of baseball and the success of their sons a delight to them. Jeff Idelson, president of the Baseball Hall of Fame, wrote a letter to Bill Bavasi, then GM of the Mariners, remembering the last time he saw Buzzie: "He was sitting on the porch, listening to the Mariners and pissed off you were losing a spring training game. He poured me a Coke, we talked about the Hall and he settled down." Buzzie died on May 1, 2008. The Bavasi family received an outpouring of affection. One writer recalled that as a college student he was doing a paper on the economics of baseball's free agency. He had written dozens of inquiry letters, but Buzzie Bavasi was the only person to respond at length—and include a sample contract. Another

Bavasi friend, Steve Corder, remembered a conversation when Buzzie was in his final year and had a sore throat. He told Corder, "At ninety-three, something has got to go wrong." Corder asked Buzzie what would be the first thing he'd say when he was reunited with Branch Rickey in heaven. Buzzie paused, then smiled and replied, "I'll ask him where the one hundred dollars is he had me give to Tommy Lasorda so Lasorda could get married." Veteran baseball scout Mel Didier—one of those scouts who live out of the limelight but embody the love of the game—wrote to Bill Bavasi: "Needless to say he was a great baseball man and one I respected a great deal. He was a BASEBALL MAN."

That capitalized encomium carries the ultimate compliment from one who has lived his life in the game of baseball to another fellow spirit. Buzzie and the Bull—baseball men. What does it mean to be a baseball man? There's an integrity to it, an earned honor that comes from working in a business that is essentially physical; the world of baseball begins with men who work with their hands. They throw balls, they catch, they bat, they run— and the men and women who inhabit their world alongside them, those who can't throw or hit or run on the green grass of the diamond, they too carry that sense of agrarian work into their jobs. Baseball begins on a field; it is never separated from an expanse of grass that holds the game in its palm. Baseball men know this and cherish it; they always have the sun in their faces and stand on the earth instead of on linoleum. To be a baseball executive and a BASEBALL MAN articulates a connection of one's soul to the field of play. Baseball men are players; they savor the stories of the game and their lives within it, and the sense of play never leaves them. In their lives they have, as Buzzie said, a thousand friends and a million laughs. Baseball men spend their lives playing a game, but it is the love of their lives.

In 1965 two baseball men intersected in the heat of a championship season. They forged a bond from laughter and conflict and friendship that was not broken until death. They played their game out that year with nerves of steel. And they came home winners.

Epilogue

Two Lives, One Team

One Sunday in the summer of 1970 during the long afternoon of a doubleheader that the Padres were losing, Bob Bavasi hurried down from the San Diego Stadium press box on an errand to the Padres clubhouse. Bob was sixteen and working for his father, Buzzie Bavasi. On this Sunday afternoon Bob rode an elevator that reminded him of a *Get Smart* set piece; it was cold and metallic and as new and soulless as the stadium. The door opened onto a concrete concourse used to deliver goods to the stadium vendors.

Off the elevator Bob took a left toward the clubhouse, but before that the runway to the dugout opened up. All of a sudden, light poured through from the ramp, and he could see outside to the green grass of the stadium. Standing in the runway, a foot up, silhouetted by the bright afternoon sunshine, leaning with a bat in one hand and holding a cigarette in the other, a circle forming between his thumb and second finger as if he were giving the okay sign, stood Al "the Bull" Ferrara.

The Bull was about to face Major League pitching but looked as relaxed as a man ready for a cocktail. He turned to young Bob, took an insouciant puff, and smiled, "Hiya, kid." Then he flicked the cigarette onto the floor and stepped back into the dugout. At that moment Bob realized that the Bull was his favorite baseball player. As a Bavasi son, he had grown up around Drysdale, Koufax, Wills—every Dodger star of the 1960s—but here was the coolest guy in the world: Al "the Bull" Ferrara, who carried a party in an empty wallet and never left a room without a smile. The Bull claimed that "If there was an off-the-field Hall of Fame, I'd be in on the first ballot," and it was probably true. In fact the Baseball Hall of Fame does contain off-the-field members. But they are not selected for the off-the-field activities the Bull was referring to.

Twenty-eight baseball executives have been voted into Cooperstown but not, for some reason, the man who had guided the Brooklyn Dodgers to their glory years of the 1950s and then led the Los Angeles Dodgers to three world championships in their first six years. Buzzie Bavasi was the architect of two decades of championship teams during baseball's golden age. He was the GM and manager of seven Hall of Fame players—and also of Al "the Bull" Ferrara.

The land of baseball is watered by rivers of stories. They encircle the game and bind it together over generations and across continents. Olympian legends populate the game: Babe Ruth eating a dozen hotdogs; Satchel Paige saying that Cool Papa Bell was so fast he could turn out the light and get into bed before it was dark; Ty Cobb sharpening his spikes with a crazed sadism; Willie Mays playing stickball in the streets of Harlem out of sheer joy. Baseball has always been an ode passed down from storyteller to storyteller. Buzzie Bavasi and Al Ferrara are both poets of the game. They appear as the obverse and reverse sides of a coin: management/player, responsible/madcap, wealthy/indebted—antithetical in their nature but welded together by their baseball stories.

The Bull sits in his Studio City apartment. He spreads his hands wide, the glint of a smile in his eyes. He explains: "Don't get me wrong; the women, the parties, the drinking—that was fun. But my first love was always baseball. Baseball was the love affair."

Now the sons of Bavasi and The Bull are all nearing retirement. The Bull wrote to Peter Bavasi, outlining his plans for his seventy-eighth birthday:

> Merry Christmas and thank you for the birthday greetings. Looking forward to Friday morning in East LA for a burrito at Al and

Bea's—lunch in Chinatown having soft shell crab Po Boy at Jewel of New Orleans—late afternoon appetizer at Eataly in Century City—capped off just for old time's sake at Mr. Chow's Beverly Hills—one cocktail at the bar with the very beautiful people. Then preparing for Christmas Eve of Seven Fishes—Christmas Day of chestnuts on an open fire—capped off by opening day at Santa Anita on December 26. But most importantly wishing you and your family a Healthy New Year—Hey Johnnnnnnny Mattei— Where is Jonnycakes?

These baseball men look back on the stories of their lives and ponder both sides of the coin. The Bull never thought for an instant about storing his grain for the winter of his life; he lived by the grace of Ferraranomics. The Bavasi family, father and sons, have been good stewards of their baseball teams, wisely accruing talent and staying within their budgets and winning championships through shrewd transactions. The Bavasis have each married once and for a long duration. Before he settled down with the woman he's lived with for over thirty-five years, the Bull was like a modern free agent of lovers, enjoying the favors of many suitors.

The Bull has lived a Fellini-like parade of adventures through the rocky shoals of an open ocean of wine, women, and song. He wrote Peter pondering the question of what-might-have-been: "Peter. . . . 30 Dewars White Label and water combined with 5 packs of cigarettes a day—oh how the mighty have fallen. The question is—if I would not have done this would I have hit higher than .259 lifetime or would I have not been able to hit at all? The Bull."

Peter's response:

Answer: Had you not had a taste for Dewars and smokes, you would not have been The Bull. You would have run with the milk-shake drinking crowd, never rolled with Pod and Zim. You might have hit .269 or maybe .249, but you might not have discovered the dogs and ponies, or Johnni Valentine or Tornado Tanja or Leta Paul; or even Baby Jane, the novelty act. The Short Stop Bar and Mario's

Marquis on Sunset might have been places you only heard about in the clubhouse but never visited. A roast in your honor would be more like a very lovely retirement dinner for Mr. Ferrara, the dedicated algebra and music teacher who, after his baseball career, spent 35 years at the Eleanor J. Toll Middle School in Glendale. The Dodgers would send an emissary to speak. So who knows? And as the Pod might say, "Screw it, Bull, let's have another cocktail and a fresh pack of Parliaments."

Sources

The main primary source for this book is a series of interviews I conducted with Al "the Bull" Ferrara over the course of two years. Ferrara, I quickly learned, has an extraordinary memory, which time and again proved to be accurate when checked against other sources. Other primary sources include interviews with the brothers Bavasi—Peter, Chris, Bill, and Bob—who spoke to me both together and separately on many occasions, as well as friends and teammates of the Bull's.

Margaret Bavasi put together an invaluable compilation of the letters Buzzie Bavasi wrote during his service in World War II. She provided context, photographs, and documentation of his unit's action, all of which made for riveting reading. Historian Mark Langill's book *Game of My Life: Dodgers* contains profiles of and first-person recollections with Buzzie Bavasi and many players of the Bavasi and Ferrara era. *Off the Record*, Buzzie Bavasi's autobiography, written with sportswriter John Strege, contains a myriad of baseball stories and Buzzie's personal history.

Baseball-Reference.com is an extraordinary source that I used frequently, double-checking individual games and specific player performances. (In virtually every case, the Bull's memory of games fifty years earlier was confirmed.)

Michael Leahy's superb book *The Last Innocents* gave a portrait of seven Dodgers of the time that is thoughtful and paints a larger picture of the culture of the 1960s. *Mover and Shaker:*

Walter O'Malley, the Dodgers, and Baseball's Westward Expansion, by Andy McCue, and *Forever Blue: The True Story of Walter O'Malley, Baseball's Most Controversial Owner, and the Dodgers of Brooklyn and Los Angeles,* by Michael D'Antonio, cover the story of the Dodgers owner and the move west.

When Buzzie Bavasi was being considered for the baseball Hall of Fame, historian Jean Ardell put together a monograph with many details of his career; this was a short-form chronology that was definitive and very useful.

I have noted below the additional books and articles that were significant resources for the individual chapters.

Introduction and Chapter 1

As with most of the text, the details of the 1965 spring training and Ferrara's road to it come from extensive interviews with Ferrara. Buzzie Bavasi's notes on how to watch a game come from a copy preserved by Bob Bavasi.

Chapter 2. Spring Training

The website Historicdodgertown.com provided additional details about the world of Dodgertown as it existed in 1965. Al Ferrara remembers Vero Beach in great detail, and his memories are backed up by recollections of Dodger players Ron Fairly, Ron Perranoski, Tommy Davis, and Wes Parker. The Bavasi family, especially Peter Bavasi, also contributed memories in several interviews.

Chapter 3. April

Throughout the book Baseball-Reference.com provided the details of individual games, down to specific at bats. A myriad of books provided information on Brooklyn and its history. Doris Kearns Goodwin's beautiful memoir, *Wait Till Next Year,* weaves personal history with the Brooklyn Dodgers of her childhood. *Brooklyn's Dodgers,* by Carl E. Prince, records the intensity of Brooklyn's connection with its team. Peter Golenbock is the author of two superb books on Brooklyn and the Dodgers: *In the Country of*

Brooklyn and *Bums: An Oral History of the Brooklyn Dodgers*. Roger Kahn's *The Boys of Summer* has long been considered the authoritative volume of the Dodgers' golden era, but some of those who were there take exception to the elegiac lace he put over the Boys of Summer after their retirement.

Chapter 4. May

Buzzie Bavasi's personal history is noted in his autobiography, *Off the Record*, written with John Strege. Margaret Bavasi provided an additional oral history and information in her unpublished compilation "Love and War in an Envelope." Margaret's compilation features the war correspondence quoted in the chapter. Ron Perranoski's memories of the Bull's home run off of Ellsworth supported Ferrara's recollection of the day.

Chapter 5. June

The definitive biography of Branch Rickey is Lee Lowenfish's *Branch Rickey: Baseball's Ferocious Gentleman*. The book is immaculately researched and authoritative. Peter Bavasi was immensely insightful in an interview about his father's approach to the job of general manager and his relationship with his scouts. Ferrara's memory of the incident on June 20 is supported by accounts in the *Los Angeles Times*, *Pasadena Independent*, and *Long Beach Independent*.

Chapter 6. July

Scott C. Roper and Stephanie Abbot Roper's article, "'We're Going to Give All We Have for This Grand Little Town': Baseball Integration and the 1946 Nashua Dodgers," published in *Historical New Hampshire*, tells the story of Buzzie Bavasi and the integration battles of 1946. Michael Leahy's *The Last Innocents* offers a thoughtful overview of the context of Los Angeles and its racial environment in the 1960s, as well as the 1965 Roseboro-Marichal fight. *The Warmth of Other Suns*, by Isabel Wilkerson, sets the world of Los Angeles and the Great Migration into a geopolitical context.

Chapter 7. August

Peter Bavasi's recollection of Ferraranomics is confirmed by Ferrara himself. Peter also gave a first-person account of the lessons Buzzie learned from Branch Rickey. John Rosengren's *The Fight of Their Lives* is the definitive account of the Roseboro-Marichal conflagration.

Chapter 8. September

Jane Leavy's *Sandy Koufax: A Lefty's Legacy* is the definitive biography of Koufax and covers his perfect game. Robert Schweppe wrote an extensive piece on the 1965 pennant race for the website Walteromalley.com. It contains both a thorough description of Koufax's perfect game and a description of the Dodger Stadium message board and its drama.

Chapter 9. October

Stew Thornley's *Minnesota Twins Baseball: Hardball History on the Prairie* covers the team's saga and the 1965 World Series. Ron Fairly and Wes Parker contributed memories of the series in interviews.

Chapter 10. Winter

Buzzie Bavasi's four-part *Sports Illustrated* article ran in May 1967 under the overall title "The Dodger Story," by Buzzie Bavasi with Jack Olsen.

Chapter 11. 1966 and Beyond

Maury Wills recounts the ill-fated Japanese goodwill tour in his autobiography *On the Run*. Ferrara's recollections of his experience on *Gilligan's Island* and *Batman* match with memories of the era from Sherwood Schwartz's son Lloyd Schwartz. Tributes to Ferrara, praising his work as a Dodger ambassador with schools and community organizations, were gathered by Bob Bavasi.

Epilogue

Bob Bavasi and Peter Bavasi provided personal recollections for this chapter.